D0604536

GTO
MOTOR
TREND

Fifty Years of MOTOR TREND

FROM THE EDITORS OF *MOTOR TREND* MAGAZINE

MBI Publishing Company

First published in 1999 by MBI Publishing Company, 729 Prospect Avenue, PO Box 1, Osceola, WI 54020-0001USA

MBI Publishing Company books are also available at discounts in bulk quantity for industrial or sales-promotional use. For details, write to Special Sales Manager at Motorbooks International Wholesalers & Distributors, 729 Prospect Avenue, PO Box 1, Osceola WI, 54020 USA.

Library of Congress Cataloging-in-Publication Data
50 Years of *Motor Trend*/the editors of *Motor Trend* magazine.
p. cm.
Includes index.
ISBN 0-7603-0781-4 (alk. paper)
1. Motor trend. 2. Automobiles. I. Motor Trend.
TL145.A16 1999
629.222—dc21 99-38863

On the frontispiece: The scientifically measured road test is a *Motor Trend* hallmark. The humble fifth-wheel is an integral tool to testing measured by hard data rather than solely subjective measures.

On the title page: By 1987, the Firebird Trans Am had matured into the GTA with a 5.7-liter/210-horsepower, Tuned Port Injected V-8 in its nose and riding on big 16-inch wheels shod with P245/50VR16 Goodyears. With a four-speed automatic doing the shifting, the GTA got to 60 miles per hour in 6.9 seconds and made an inevitable comparison with a car like the 1967 GTO.

On the front flap: After watching innumerable kit-carmakers copy his original creation, Carroll Shelby "uncovered" some unused chassis components and started up his Cobra 427 production line once again. With at least 425 horsepower aboard and the ability to corner at 1.02 g, the "continuation" Cobra, built to S/C "Semi-Competition" specs and priced at a blinding $500,000, performed significantly better than had the Cobra 427 (non-S/C) tested by *MT* back in '66.

On the back flap: A full 14 years after its debut, the Porsche 959 remains, arguably, the most technologically advanced production automobile ever built. Only 200 copies of the 959 were built at a price of $130,000 each and none was certified to operate on American roads. Considering how the 959 was built, even at that price, it's assumed Porsche took a loss on every car.

On the back cover: **Top:** The updated 1999 Ford Mustang sandwiched by two of 1969's hottest musclecars: a 335-horsepower Mach 1 428 Cobra Jet and George Follmer's 470-horsepower Boss 302 Trans Am racer.
Bottom: 1997 Corvette**:** Three years after *MT*'s first report on its engineering and development, it was finally time to drive the C5 Corvette with its new 5.7-liter/345-horsepower all-aluminum OHV LS1 V-8, rear-mounted six-speed transaxle, and vastly improved structure and practicality.

Printed in Hong Kong

Contents

FOREWORD

Motor Trend's humble beginnings came from two men's passion for cars. In 1949, 23-year-old hot rodder and fledgling publisher Bob Petersen teamed with his friend, Walt Woron, to create an entirely new kind of car magazine.

Their dream was to test every make and model of car, import and domestic. They also strived to cover every trend: racing, customs, hot rods, economy cars, luxury cars, family cars, pickup trucks, campers, and more. Their legacy was the creation of a scientific road-testing process and the founding of the world-renowned Car of the Year award.

In 1949, the postwar boom was carrying the country headlong into the American Dream era, where bigger V-8s, more chrome, and taller tailfins were the scorecards of automotive status. In this car crazy atmosphere, Pete and Walt's formula helped *Motor Trend* quickly grow to become the world's largest circulation car magazine.

Over the past 50 years, *MT*'s editors have tested thousands of cars, written millions of words, and helped inform and entertain three generations of car enthusiasts. Thank you Bob Petersen, Walt Woron, and all the great people from *MT*'s storied history, for creating an oft-imitated, but never equaled, American publishing icon. It's where I've wanted to work since age ten.

—C. Van Tune, Editor-in-Chief, *Motor Trend* magazine

INTRODUCTION

Why *Motor Trend*?

Motor Trend is always growing. From the moment it was born, it's been dedicated not only to reporting on the motoring world's trends, but to bringing to light those innovations that would inspire trends. A half-century into its life, *Motor Trend* is still dynamic, still dedicated to its mission, and still very, very young.

Back in 1948, Robert E. Petersen started his first magazine, *Hot Rod*. Though *Hot Rod* was an immediate hit, some advertisers were put off by hot rodding's "outlaw" image. They'd advertise, all right, if Petersen were to change the magazine's name. That, of course, was unthinkable. Instead, Petersen launched *Motor Trend* as a more upscale magazine for enthusiasts as interested in production vehicles as in modifying older ones.

"We weren't satisfied with just another magazine," wrote *Motor Trend*'s first editor, Walt Woron, in *Motor Trend*'s opening issue back in September 1949. "We wanted a magazine that would interest the foreign car exponent, the custom car fan, and also be equally interesting to the stock car owner. For a title, we wanted a name that would not only be catchy, but one to tell you what it is about.

"That's the 'why' of *Motor Trend*—a magazine that brings you the trends of the automotive field: designs of the future, what's new in motoring, news from the Continent, trends in design. *Motor Trend* will also feature photographs of well-designed custom cars, foreign cars, and unusual race cars—you'll read about horseless carriages and patented automotive inventions that were never produced."

Petersen and company couldn't have picked a more propitious time than 1949 to launch a new automotive magazine. In the previous 20 years, the United States had survived a devastating economic depression and fought an unbelievably brutal second world war. Long accustomed to deprivation, Americans were once again confident in their country's abilities and optimistic about future progress. They were tough people who had paid their dues and deserved some reward for their substantial sacrifices.

Before the war, cars had been for the very rich or were very utilitarian. While the first civilian postwar vehicles were barely warmed-over prewar models, almost all the '49 models were new from the ground up. And they were designed to offer the middle class the sorts of features once reserved only for the wealthy. In the new consumer-driven world, cars were the most obvious middle-class status symbol.

In essence, the 100 or so years of automobiles can be divided roughly into pre– and post–World War II eras. *Motor Trend*, better and more diligently than any other magazine, has been the chronicler of that second era. And now, fully embracing today's technology and tomorrow's possibilities, it's ready to further that narrative into another millennium.

MOTOR trend
the magazine for a motoring world
TWENTY FIVE CENTS
SEPTEMBER 1949

1

THE 1950s

1949–1959

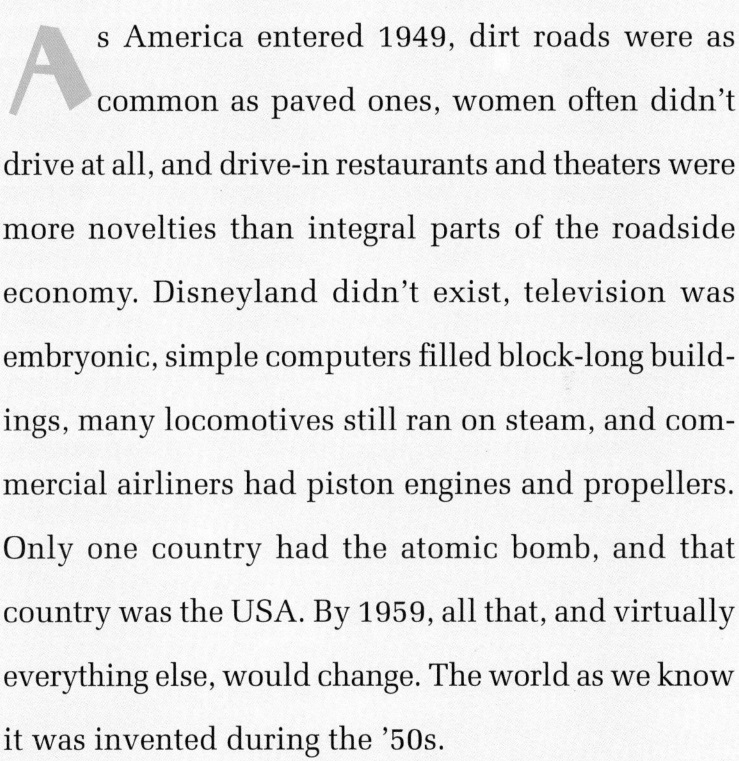

As America entered 1949, dirt roads were as common as paved ones, women often didn't drive at all, and drive-in restaurants and theaters were more novelties than integral parts of the roadside economy. Disneyland didn't exist, television was embryonic, simple computers filled block-long buildings, many locomotives still ran on steam, and commercial airliners had piston engines and propellers. Only one country had the atomic bomb, and that country was the USA. By 1959, all that, and virtually everything else, would change. The world as we know it was invented during the '50s.

No car more epitomizes the excesses of '50s styling trends than the '59 Cadillac, with the most flamboyant tailfins ever seen. The Series 62 sedan here was the division's mainstay.

Motor Trend's first issue wore the promise that it was "the magazine for a motoring world" and a September 1949 date on its cover. What it shared with the rest of that world was a passion for the new, an absolute enthusiasm for a future that seemed limitless and exciting. And no place was more enthralled with the future or with cars than Los Angeles, California, the town that has always been *Motor Trend's* home.

The first car featured in the magazine was the Kurtis Sports Car, which contained at least as many innovations as any car then in production. Using a series of standard componentry and his innate engineering abilities, race-car builder, Frank Kurtis, constructed a road car that foreshadowed many of the developments *Motor Trend* would cover over the next decade. The Los Angeles–built Kurtis Sports Car prototype used a welded steel structure, integrating many body components to add strength, was finished in fiberglass panels, was powered by a supercharged Studebaker engine, and used side windows made of that wartime wonder material, Plexiglas. Ultimately, the Kurtis Sports Car wasn't a success (only 36 were built). But it was the perfect vehicle to launch *Motor Trend.*

NOVEMBER 1949 ▲

Car of the Year: The 1949 Cadillac

Motor Trend's first Car of the Year was chosen by writer John Bond as the most significant advance of the year, though the formal award of the "Car of the Year" honor was still years away.

"The new Cadillac is the first evidence in the U.S. of a trend toward OHV (overhead-valve) engines, a trend noticeable even before the war in Europe. In Europe since the war, not one of the large number of new or redesigned engines is a side valve ('L' head) engine. A General Motors executive recently stated to the press that all GM cars would have OHV engines in the new future."

With Editor Walt Woron at the helm, *Motor Trend's* first issues were devoted more to the world of custom cars and the emerging racing world than the road tests that would eventually become the magazine's most definitive feature. Articles were devoted to "Restyling a '41 Buick" or showcasing the forward-looking illustrations of Col. Alexis de Sakhnoffsky. It wasn't until the December 1949 issue, *Motor Trend's* fourth, that a road test appeared, a "Motor Trials" report on the '50 Buick Special.

But *Motor Trend's* signature feature was launched even before its first road test. In the November 1949 issue, automotive enthusiast John Bond named the Cadillac "Car of the Year." In an editor's note, Woron explained Bond's assignment simply: "In this article, automotive enthusiast John Bond was asked to describe his idea of the most advanced of the '49 models. Before making his selection, he considered all the models, ranging from the Jeepster through the Lincoln, and gave serious thought to the engine, appearance and handling characteristics. His final choice may be subject to controversy, but definitely has merit."

As obvious as it may seem in retrospect, *Motor Trend* didn't quite realize the lightning it had bottled with the Car of the Year idea. After John Bond's rather informal "Car of the Year" '49 article, the phrase wouldn't be used again until 1951 when Chrysler earned "Car of the Year." It wasn't until 1956 that the formal "1st Annual *Motor Trend* Award" was announced and not until 1958 when that award evolved into the familiar Car of the Year honor (won that year by the four-passenger '58 Ford Thunderbird).

The '50s were full of innovations that would revolutionize the automotive world and some that would just fizzle. As early as May 1950, *Motor Trend* was exploring the possibility of turbine power for cars. In October of that same year, it investigated the potential of fiberglass body construction. The world probably still isn't ready for an atomic-powered car, but *Motor Trend* pondered the idea way back in April 1951. It was tough to get a TV set into a living room in 1952, but MT was already engineering ways to install one in a car that year. (In 1999, Oldsmobile became the first to offer onboard video as a factory option.) Fuel injection got a thorough going-over in the September 1954 issue. In August 1957, the magazine was "Testing the potentialities of the Latham supercharger," while in November of that year, it featured "Your Flying Car of the Future."

Besides the thrill of speculating about what was yet to come, *Motor Trend* also developed a strong tradition of practical consumer advice during the '50s. Fuel economy runs were a perennial in the magazine, and the October 1953 issue carried a report on the emergence of self-service gas stations. In April 1954, writer Paul Everton shared how to re-cover door panels, Al Kidd explained how to install a radio in the July 1955 issue, and a June 1957 article shared just what to expect from a new paint job.

Racing grew steadily through the decade, and *Motor Trend* was there at every step. The first issue told readers what to expect at "A Sunday Gymkhana for Sports Cars," and by the second issue, editor Woron actively lobbied for the construction of road racing courses in the West. Coverage of the Indianapolis 500 in *Motor Trend* was always extensive, and by 1951, the magazine was also reporting on the fast growth of NASCAR stock car racing in the Southeast. Whatever the variation, *Motor Trend* was eager to report each new racing development.

While Jack Kerouac was writing "On the Road," *Motor Trend* was reporting from the road. Big adventures like November 1952's "I Smuggled a Car Out of Russia" got prominent placement in the magazine, while smaller portraits of the world were featured in "Driving Around with Walt Woron."

Unfettered by government regulation, the '50s was a giddy time of automotive experimentation and progress. It's the era when *Motor Trend* matured into the world's authoritative automotive resource.

DECEMBER 1949 ▶

Motor Trials: Factory Testing the Buick Special

Motor Trend's first road test was of the '50 Buick Special.

"A fundamental difference between driving a Buick Special without Dynaflow and one with Dynaflow is in the absence of a clutch pedal. However the emergency brake pedal is placed in approximately the same location as that previously occupied by the clutch pedal. If you accidentally hit this pedal while driving the car, you apply the emergency brake. It is then necessary to pull out on the emergency knob control, placed below the left side of the instrument panel. The advantage of this type of control, however, is its use for hill-holding."

1950

It is a certainty that our automotive engineers will devote much time and study to the development of the gas turbine. And we, whether we be engineers, technicians, or laymen, should view this, if not optimistically, then at least with an open mind.

—*"Things To Come"*
May 1950

MAY 1950

Motor Trials: Testing the Economy-Minded 1950 Mercury

The '50 Mercury is now remembered as the base for thousands of "lead sled" low riders and as a design classic, not as an economy car. *"Returning the '50 Mercury to the factory after eight hours on the road, having traveled 120 miles on open highway, over mountainous terrain, and through city streets, we felt the Mercury had lived up to its advance billing. It is a car that any owner could well be proud of."*

1950

JUNE 1950 ▲

Motor Trials: Nash Revives a Famous Name in the New Rambler

Motor Trend's first recorded adventure in dirt was taking a fully loaded '50 Nash Rambler up this steep dirt road.

"The Nash Rambler is a comfortable car—the more you drive it, the more you like it. And probably, outside of its good performance, one of its chief selling points will be the fact that it is the lowest-priced five-passenger convertible available on the market today. Priced below today's convertibles, this car includes in its standard equipment such items as an air heater, radio, directional signals, clock, foam rubber cushions, and other extras."

1950

SEPTEMBER 1950 ▲

Motor Trials: Chevrolet

Editor Walt Woron compared the manual transmission '50 Chevy with the new Powerglide two-speed automatic-equipped version. Included was the subheading, "*MT* Editor Prefers Chevrolet with Conventional Transmission Over Powerglide."

"Definitely designed for the person who wants to drive without shifting, the Powerglide nonetheless has the disadvantage of not allowing the driver to select a lower gear by depressing the throttle as in other automatic transmissions. It is possible, however, to shift the control lever from 'drive' to 'low' and vice versa, but if a transmission is 'automatic,' this should not be necessary."

1950

NOVEMBER 1950 ▲

Road Jet: Speed and Power Combined in New Muntz Car

A development of the Kurtis Sports Car featured in *Motor Trend's* first issue, the Muntz was financed by famed TV pitchman Earl "Madman" Muntz and built at the Kurtis-Kraft facility in Los Angeles. Walt Woron toured the factory and sat down for a round-table discussion with Earl Muntz and Frank Kurtis.

"Question: Mr. Kurtis, I notice the similarity between your Kurtis Sports Car and the Muntz Road Jet. Is the Road Jet a conversion of the original car?
Answer: In a manner of speaking, it is, but it has major refinements.
Question: What are some of these major refinements?
Answer: Longer wheelbase, Cadillac engine, four-passenger, metal removable top.
Question: What do you consider to be the car's best features?
Answer: Its balance, low center of gravity, low sitting position, and of course the short wheelbase which all add up to better handling."

1951

Some scientists are not yet ready to acknowledge that atomic-powered automobiles will ever be a reality, or that there is any economic necessity for such transportation. From the standpoint of present-day information there is much to be said for their arguments.

—"Atomic Power in Your Car"
April 1951

FEBRUARY 1951 ▸

Motor Trials: Packard 200 Is the One to Beat for Comfort and Performance

Packard was already only a shadow of its former self in 1951, and merged with Studebaker in 1954. By 1958, Packard was out of the car business. *"We've been exposed to manufacturer's claims and enthusiasm for a long enough time to look upon them with some reservation, and this was naturally so in the case of the '51 Packard. But now that the motor trial of the Packard 200 with the Ultramatic is a thing of the past, we know why the Packard Motor Company is so enthused about its product. The Packard test car was a 200 series with the 138-horsepower engine and Ultramatic transmission. Usually any Packard is thought of as a large car, but the model we tested is affectionately called the 'baby' by the Packard people, having a wheelbase of only 122 inches. Even so, the car is still a big car."*

1951

JANUARY 1951 ▲

Motor Trials: Ford with Fordomatic Is a Top Performer

Testing the '51 Ford before it was available to the public, *Motor Trend* cleverly disguised the updated appearance with newspaper and masking tape before it left Ford's Long Beach, California, assembly plant.

"The acceleration of the '51 Ford with Fordomatic doesn't exactly pin you to your seat, but it has more-than-average speed up and down the scale. In a test against a '50 Ford with conventional transmission and 4.10:1 rear axle, the two cars stayed practically even from 0-60 mph and for standing start quarter mile. One major improvement has been made in regard to the '51 Ford's front seat. As the seat is adjusted fore-and-aft, the seatback pivots at the lower end, bringing the top closer to your shoulders or moving it away as the case may be. One common complaint still evident, however, is that the right side of the seat doesn't hold well in its track."

1951

MARCH 1951 ▲

Motor Trials: Hudson Hornet Fastest Yet Tested—97.5 mph!

In the early years of NASCAR, no car dominated stock car racing like the Hudson Hornet. It impressed *Motor Trend* as well, zipping to 60 mph in a then-impressive 14.6 seconds and hitting a top speed of 97.5 mph. Herb Thomas, driving Marshall Teague's "Fabulous Hudson Hornet," won both the 1951 and 1953 NASCAR Grand National championships driving Hornets, with Tim Flock taking the title in 1952 in yet another Hudson. In 1954, Thomas won 12 races in the Hudson, even though Lee Petty took the championship driving a Chrysler.

"If you've ever seen a Hudson after it has been involved in an accident (or have seen photographs of one), you've seen the greatest advantage to the unit-type, all-welded frame and body, such as used on the Hornet. The Monobuilt frame completely encircles the passengers, front, sides and rear, while the floor is recessed below the frame. The safety aspect of this arrangement cannot be denied, while the merits of the 'step-down' floor are dependent on personal likes and human configurations."

1951

JUNE 1951

Motor Trials: Studebaker V-8 a Terrific Surprise

Besides achieving an 18.1-second 0-60-mph clocking, the 120-horsepower Studebaker V-8 was the first car ever to be seen in *Motor Trend* burning down its rear tires. That smoky tradition has expanded ever since.

"According to all indications, the Studebaker Corporation should be able to sell all the V-8s they can build. They can't miss, offering the public such a package of power and comfort for the money. We were so impressed with the performance of the Commander that we feel no qualms whatsoever in making this prediction."

1952

The civilian Jeep is proving itself as valuable and versatile to the sportsman as its army prototype was to the military.

—*"Unique Cars for Sportsmen"*
October 1952

JULY 1952 ▶

MT Research Tests the 1952 Firedome DeSoto

Chrysler's legendary "Hemi" V-8, a name derived from the hemispherical shape of its combustion chambers, was first tested way back in the '52 DeSoto.

"DeSoto's V-8 renders with ease 160 horsepower from a mere 273 cubic inches. In spite of all its parts being lightly stressed, in spite of a 'low' compression ratio of 7.1:1, it leads the industry (all full-size cars) in power developed per cubic inch of displacement and does it on regular-grade gasoline, no premium. The '52 DeSoto is a car of many contradictions: It has one of the world's best and most modern engines; its transmission keeps that engine from doing its best work; the engine that sets the pace for tomorrow propels a body that's tied to the past."

1952

APRIL 1952

Ferrari: Enzo's V-12s Are Building a Speed Legend in the Postwar World

Motor Trend's Michael Brown took an early look at budding supercar maker Ferrari and the marque's Modena production facility.

"Enzo's judgment proved unerring in every way. He laid the foundation of his stable with first things first: the finest mechanics he could find, admitting that these unsung heroes are the primary source of victory. Next came the obvious heroes—the drivers. Enzo gathered the greatest talent about him: Nuvolari, Trossi, Farina, Pintacuda, Brivio, Varzi, Chiron, Sommer, Villoresi for a few. And, of course, the conductor of this thundering symphony orchestra was Ferrari himself."

1953

Ideas from Europe for Customizing Your Car

MOTOR TREND

The Car Owners Magazine
Combined with Auto Sportsman

Those Shocking Seat Covers

OCTOBER 1953 25c

7 ECONOMY CARS

Analyzed, tested, reported on—so you can determine which car is your best buy

Miniature powerplants and fabulous gas mileage don't often mix with surplus power.

—*"Analysis of Seven Economy Cars"*
October 1953

JULY 1953 ▶

America's Economy Classic

Editor Walt Woron and Bob Scollay participated in the 1953 Mobilgas Economy Run to find out how to squeeze the best possible mileage out of a stock Packard.

"One trick, employed by all the drivers, will save gas but is not productive for good overall car economy. This practice consists of getting the car in motion as soon as the engine starts. These cold starts, made before the engine oil is warm and circulated throughout the engine, can produce expensive wear and tear. Other extreme efforts to aid gas mileage, such as obtaining wind velocity and direction data during the run, are obviously applicable to a contest and daily driving."

JULY 1953 ◀

Descendent of the Devilfish

Glen Hire and Vernon Antoine of Whittier, California, built the fiberglass-bodied Manta Ray in their garage, based on a '51 Studebaker V-8 chassis. There's no record of the Manta Ray going into production.

"The 4200 hours of work that went into this car have paid off, for Hire and Antoine are now planning production schedules, and their garage-workshop will soon be a landlocked breeding place for these four-wheeled denizens of the deep."

1953

NOVEMBER 1953 ▲

Walt Woron Tests the First Corvette

Motor Trend's first test of the '53 Corvette found a car with only a 150-horsepower 235-cubic inch straight-six for power and a two-speed automatic transmission. So the first Corvette took 11.5 seconds to go 0-60 mph.

"Probably one of the biggest surprises I got with the car was when I took it through some sharp corners at fairly good speeds. I'd heard that Chevrolet had designed the suspension so that it would stay flat and stick in corners, but I took it with several grains of salt. It sticks better than some foreign sports cars I've driven."

1954

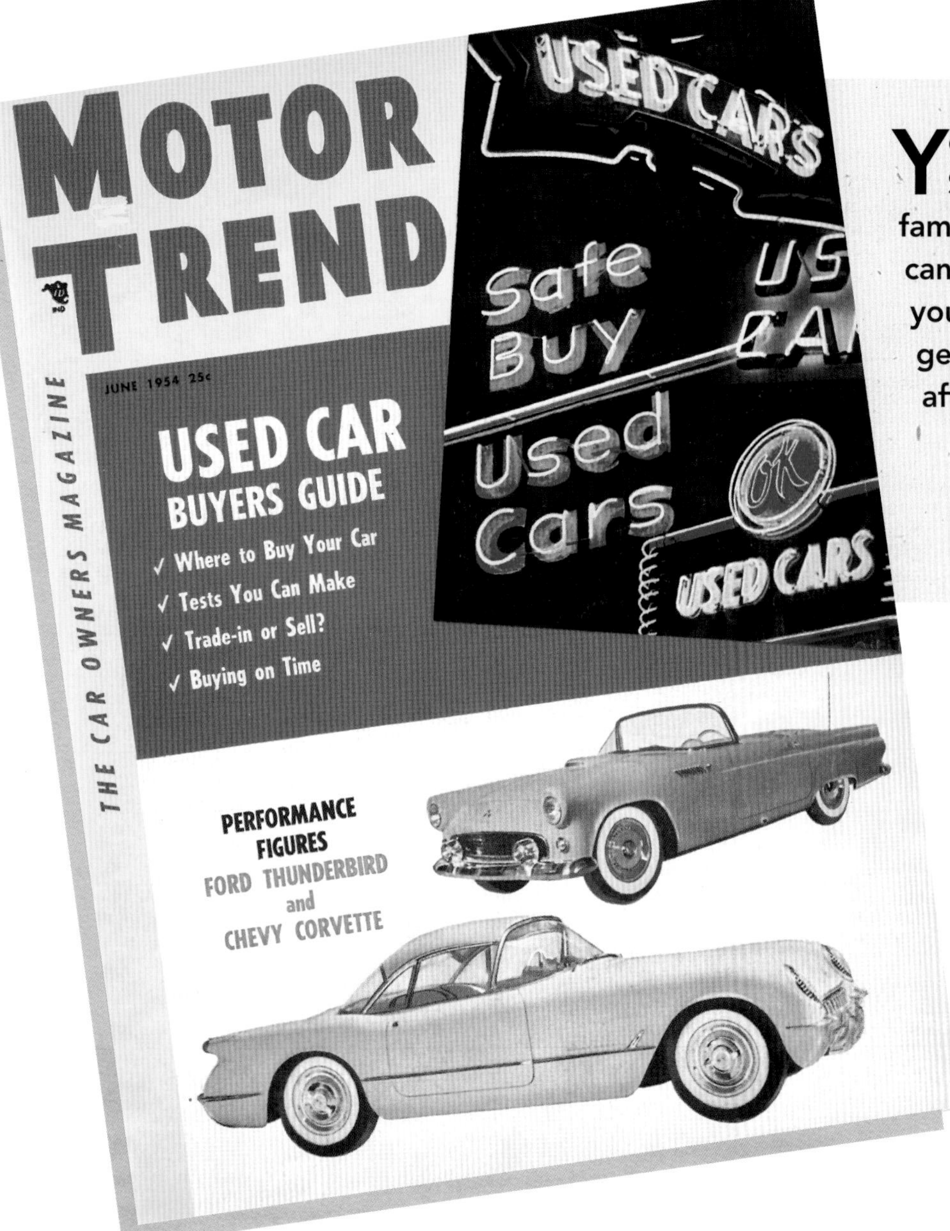

You don't want a 1931 Plymouth? You have $800, and you just want a good, comfortable family sedan? So much the better. You certainly can find one for your money (especially now) and you can find one you'll be proud of, one you'll get a bang out of driving, and one that you can afford to support after you've bought it.

—"How to Get the Used Car You Want"
June 1954

SEPTEMBER 1954 ▶

Station Wagon Trek

MT tested six station wagons ranging from the Chevy Handyman to the Willys Jeep Four-Wheel-Drive. On the cover was this Ford Mainline Ranch Wagon stuffed with gear.

"There are many nice features about the Ford, but it falls short in comparison to the compactness of the Plymouth, the looks of the Stude, the utility of the Jeep. Yet it's a good compromise, having a little of each of these features. Plus outstanding handling."

1954

1954

1954

◄ APRIL 1954

MT Previews: Mercedes-Benz 300SL

To many, the Mercedes 300SL "Gullwing" coupe, with its distinctive top-hinged doors, remains the greatest sports car of the postwar era.

"There's magic in the name Mercedes. Few of us have ever been fortunate to drive a Mercedes, and many people have never even seen one; but to most of us, the name is almost legend. If slightly less than $7000 will satisfy your curiosity, you can park a new 300SL in your garage and explore its innermost secrets to your heart's content. The 300SL is described as capable of moving over the 160-mph mark, and able to turn 0-100 mph in 19 seconds, 0-60 in 9. Its power comes from a six-cylinder, 240-horsepower engine utilizing an overhead camshaft and a highly developed fuel-injection system."

OCTOBER 1954 ▲

MT Road Test: 1954 Buick Special

The new-in-'54 Buicks featured a wraparound windshield, and even the low-line Special adopted the V-8 engine the division had introduced in '53.

"Take the Buick's appearance this year: Admittedly, the Buick line has the industry's newest look. Though startled at first, the public has now accepted Buick's wraparound windshield and dropped waistline, its lowness and squareness of body, its compact yet impressive look. Let's compare our actual test figures of this year's Special V-8 with last year's Special inline eight. The '54 car, with 18 more horses, came out ahead in acceleration, beating the '53 in the quarter mile by 1.1 seconds; in the 0-60 test, the '54 car's time was better by 4.2 seconds."

1955

Are trucks one of the proving grounds for engineering innovations on passenger cars? Here are some new truck developments.

—*Table of Contents, "Truck Trends"*
July 1955

JANUARY 1955 ▶

_MT_ Research Road Test: 1955 Chevrolet V-8

No engine has been produced in greater quantity than Chevrolet's legendary "small block" V-8. It entered production displacing 265 cubic inches and rated at 162 horsepower, and it was inserted into the nearly as fabled '55 Chevy, where it traipsed 0-60 mph in 12.3 seconds. Produced in factory versions displacing up to 400 cubic inches, it became the most successful engine in racing history. The small block finally left production at the end of the '99 model year when the last of GM's C/K-based Tahoe, Yukon, and Suburban SUVs rolled off the line. Considering the hobby it launched, MT's comment in a caption may be the biggest understatement in the magazine's history.

"If you like to putter around your new car, or if you really take it apart, Chevy ranks high as a promising weekend hobby."

1955

DECEMBER 1954 ▸

Driving Around With Walt Woron

No car is more an icon of the '50s than the two-seat Ford Thunderbird produced between 1955 and 1957. Ford will produce a new two-seat Thunderbird in 2000 as a 2001 model.

"Ford prefers to call it a 'personal car.' The thinking behind this, as brought out in a discussion with W.R. Burnett, chief passenger car engineer for Ford, is that, 'although the Thunderbird has the performance and attributes of most sports cars, management also felt it should have a few more comforts to make it more appealing to a wider segment of the public.' "

1955

AUGUST 1955 ▲

Boredom at the Brickyard

The odds weren't just against Bill Vukovich in the 1955 race, so was fate. On the 56th lap, he was involved in a crash with four other cars and lost his life. Bob Sweikert won in the A.J. Watson–tuned John Zink Special.

"Many people almost overlooked the excellent winning performance by these two men. Mechanic A.J. Watson had the Zink car in winning tune and it ran flawlessly. Despite his fine No. 6 ranking among AAA drivers in 1954, Bob Sweikert was an outsider at Indy. After his beautifully driven 500, he'll be a favorite."

DECEMBER 1955 ▲

The 1956 Chryslers

At the end of '55 the first '56 Chryslers, including this DeSoto Firedome, hit showrooms packing the newest innovation, the pushbutton automatic transmission. Gimmick or not, the last Chrysler product with a pushbutton transmission was produced in 1964.

"When I first heard about Chrysler's revolutionary pushbutton transmission, I formed the opinion that, here at last, was 'a gimmick to end all gimmicks'—something on which to pin sales pitches about 'pushbutton driving—change gears with the tip of a finger.' After driving the '56 Chrysler cars (all have it) with this pushbutton control, though, I'm convinced it's far more than a gimmick."

1956

The Year's BIGGEST Step Forward

MOTOR TREND

MT presents its automotive award to the car manufacturer making the most significant advancement of 1956

ROAD TESTS: CHRYSLER PONTIAC

MAY 1956 25c

Road Test HOW DOES VOLKSWAGEN COMPARE?

ANALYZING THE GROWING VOLKSWAGEN FAMILY

The completed car, unlike some of the other GM dream cars, is completely functional in every detail. Tailfins are a characteristic Cadillac trademark. Dual headlights provide efficient road lighting. Outer lights are flat beam city lights; the inner ones are highly penetrating highway lights. Both sets are automatically controlled by Autronic Eye.

—*"Exit: Dream, Enter: Reality"*
April 1955

1956

JUNE 1956 ▲

1956 Thunderbird and Corvette Road Test

Ford may have called its Thunderbird a "personal car," but its natural competitor was still the Corvette, Detroit's only other mass-produced two-seater. The 312-cubic inch, 215-horsepower V-8 in the Ford zipped the T-Bird 0-60 in 11.5 seconds and completed the quarter mile in 18.0 seconds at 76.5 mph. The 265-cubic-inch, dual-quad 240-horse Chevy V-8, had the Corvette doing those same tricks in 11.6 seconds and 17.9 seconds at 77.5 mph.

"The Thunderbird is pretty much what Ford claims it is—a 'personal car,' suitable for the bachelor, for the young or 'young in heart' couple, or the husband or wife as a second car. The Corvette is less of a personal car and closer to being, or easily becoming, a sports car. The sales philosophy of Chevrolet seems to have been more to compete with the foreign sports car market—at least until the Thunderbird came along. Which one for you? Within $2.60, you can have your choice. Each performs a slightly different function, and each does right well for itself."

1956

AUGUST 1956 ▲

1956 Cadillac

In the 1950s, Cadillacs were the ultimate automotive dream cars for Americans. Look closely and you'll see that this Eldorado is actually a customized '56 Chevy. In '57, Cadillac would adopt an "X-frame" design that significantly lowered its cars' silhouettes and the fins would grow even grander.

1956

Test Equipment in the 1950s ▲

Before the advent of electronic timing and recording equipment, *Motor Trend's* acceleration testing was done with two men (and they were always men) aboard. One would drive, while the other would trigger a series of stopwatches as different speeds were reached according to a certified speedometer measuring the revolutions of a "fifth wheel" temporarily bolted to the rear bumper.

1957

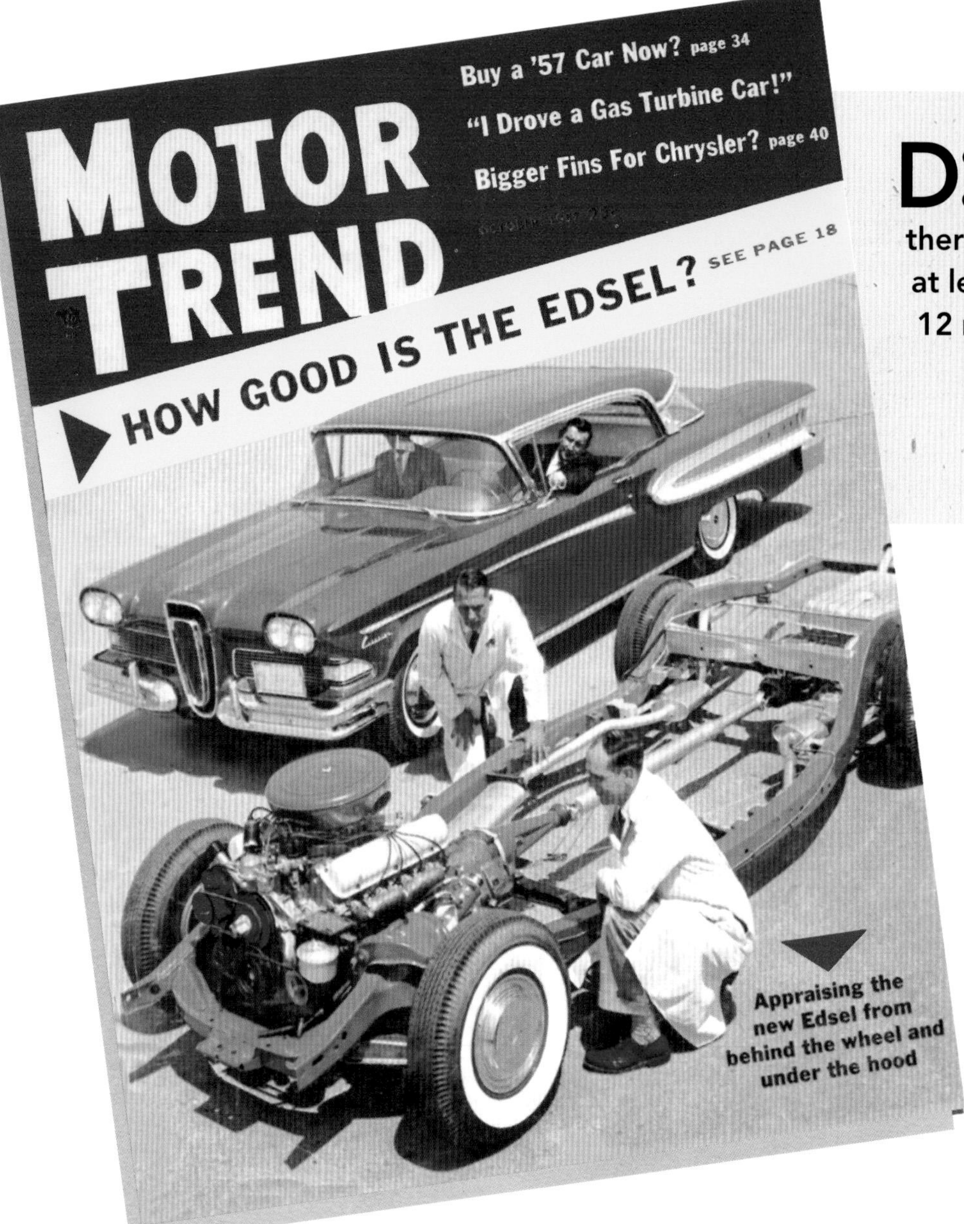

Definitely a cut apart from the majority of cars, it is extremely doubtful whether there will be a style remotely like the Edsel, at least in most components, within the next 12 months.

—*"How Good Is the Edsel?"*
October 1957

AUGUST 1957 ▸

500-Horsepower Four-Cam V-8

Bob Gillelan, a machinist with Moldex Tool Company in Detroit, handbuilt this four-cam engine, which made it onto *Motor Trend's* cover. Though based on a '53 Chrysler block, the engine was essentially handbuilt, using components from various manufacturers including, for example, '55 Ford valve guides. With an 11.3:1 compression ratio, Gillelan expected 500 horsepower to be produced. *"Engines like this one take months to build—and this is a spare time mill, too. As it stands now, the engine has consumed better than 10 months of work, and the end, though in sight, has not quite been achieved."*

1957

MARCH 1957

Chrysler 300-C

Chrysler introduced its 300-series "letter" cars in 1955, powered by the amazing Hemi engine, and immediately dominated NASCAR stock car racing. But it wasn't until the appearance of the Virgil Exner-designed, 375-horsepower, '57 300-C that many feel the series fully blossomed as luxurious performance machines. The letter series reappeared for 1999 as the 300-M which earned *Motor Trend's* Car of the Year honor.

"Cubic inches, pure and simple, are the most direct route to super performance. For 1957, the 300-C is up in displacement from last year's 354 to 392 by means of both greater bore and stroke. The standard heads of the 300-C have a compression ratio of 9.25:1, hemispherical chambers as previously and induction is by means of dual four-throat carburetors. This is probably one of the most comfortable cars available today. The firmer springing not only reduces almost to the elimination point the danger of bottoming on sharp dips and rise, but overall control of the cars is similarly improved."

JUNE 1957

A.C. Bristol

The 2.0-liter, six-cylinder-powered A.C. Bristol is little remembered in the United States. The major exception would be that Carroll Shelby would install Ford V-8s in the car during the '60s to create his Cobra.

"Aluminum paneling is used on the handbuilt body and shows excellent workmanship. The base price of $5195 for the A.C. Bristol ensures a quality automobile for the discerning motorist and a high-performing sports car for the eager, competition-minded driver."

1958

They quit making Buicks when 1958 production stopped. Now they're building automobiles.

—"The 1959 Buick on Trial"
October 1958

JANUARY 1958 ▲

Plymouth, Chevrolet, Ford: On Trial

No rivalry is, or has been, more heated than that between Plymouth, Ford, and Chevrolet. Four-wheels off the ground wasn't part of testing the Ford Fairlane. In 0-60-mile per hour times, the 300-horsepower Ford's 10.2-second clocking was only third best. The 280-horse Chevy managed a 9.1-second time for the same feat, and the 305-horsepower Plymouth scorched the track with a 7.7-second performance.

"When you select one car of any one make as its representative, you are subject to error, for any one car of any one make can be only the norm; others may be better or worse. Then when you compare three different cars against the other and derive from this conclusions that apply to all cars of each of these makes, you are on dangerous ground."

1958

FEBRUARY 1958 ▶

1958 Thunderbird

Ford redesigned the Thunderbird for '58 around a unibody structure and seats for four passengers. While the '55 to '57 two-seat T-Birds are today considered the most collectible, the four-seat "square birds" were far more popular with the buying public. Ford sold 21,380 '57 T-Birds and 37,892 of the '58s. The '58 was also impressive enough to earn *Motor Trend's* Car of the Year honor.
"Widest doors in the industry," says Ford, and I believe them. Seems almost like pulling a side (48.8 inches of it) off the car. Duck a little to get in, or better yet use the sports car technique of backing into the front seats. This is where comfort begins. Each of the four seats (two separates in front and two-in-one for the rear) is an honest-to-goodness bucket job. Soft springs in the center and back allow your body to drop into (rather than sit on) the cushions. Then you become conscious of foam rubber cushion edges which ride up around your thighs and back to provide the most comforting support of all '58s. As one engineer said, 'It's almost like riding with someone's arms around you.' (How nice.)"

OCTOBER 1958 ◀

Toyopet Crown

Toyota had been around for a while, but was a newcomer to the U.S. when *MT* tested the Toyopet Crown sedan powered by a 60-horsepower, four-cylinder engine.
"While it may never win any stoplight Grand Prix (it wasn't intended to), neither will it come unglued at the seams on the first washboard road. This strength factor is a necessity in Japan where roads are notoriously rugged. Any automobile which is not several degrees more rugged than its roadway is going to fall apart. (We personally know of a popular American make which has a life expectancy of less than six months on Japan's back roads)".

1959

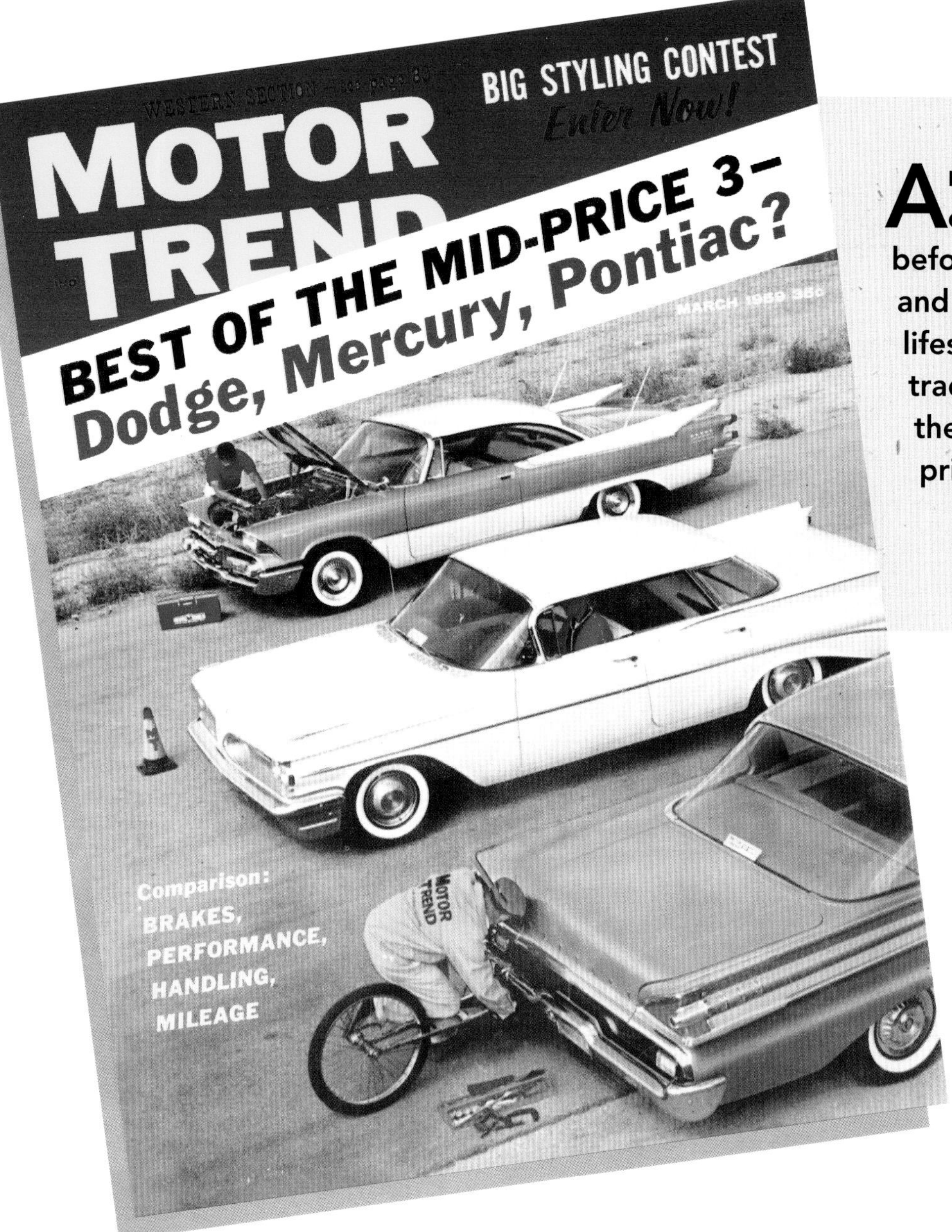

MOTOR TREND
BIG STYLING CONTEST
Enter Now!
MARCH 1959 35c
BEST OF THE MID-PRICE 3—
Dodge, Mercury, Pontiac?
Comparison:
BRAKES,
PERFORMANCE,
HANDLING,
MILEAGE

A man in the 1960s has a good chance of copping a ride in a military aerial Jeep before living out his traditional three score and ten. And if fortune smiles and his lifespan is continued a few years beyond tradition, he may even enjoy flitting about the country at treetop height in his privately owned flymobile.

—*"Spotlight on Detroit"*
March 1959

1959

APRIL 1959

Porsche/Corvette

MT would come back to explore the rivalry between Germany's Porsche and America's Corvette over and over again. In 1959, both were priced around $4,000, but there was a great disparity in power. The brawny Corvette was tested with a 250-horsepower 283-cubic inch V-8 aboard. The Porsche had only 70 horses emerging from its 1,588-cubic-centimeter (96.5-cubic inch) flat four, which meant that, while the Corvette bounded 0-60 mph in just 7.8 seconds, it took the Porsche a full 15.2 seconds to reach that velocity. *"If getting a lot of performance from a precision-built, small-displacement engine is intriguing, the Porsche is the answer. If you like the idea of having one of the world's fastest accelerating sports cars, then pick the Corvette. MT staff members became extremely partisan—on both sides of the fence. Feelings were evenly divided except for one nameless male who refused to choose, insisting he would be happy only with both cars."*

1959

NOVEMBER 1958 ▲

Who'll Be Top Dog in 1959?

Following up on the January 1958 comparison test, *MT* returned to assess the '59 Plymouth, Ford, and Chevy in November, this time being more affirmative in its decisions. The Plymouth won for "best-riding suspension," "best-handling suspension," "most novel accessory" for its electronic mirror, "most body options," and "best front suspension." Chevy took honors for "most changed body style," "best brakes," "best interior (standard model)," "most quiet ride (wind noise)," and "best rear suspension." Ford earned "best attempt at fuel economy," "best steering (mechanical)," "newest mechanical feature" for its two-speed transmission, and "heaviest frame."

"Each manufacturer believes his product is the best, but unlike the automotive journalist, he cannot drive his competitor's test cars—at least before public introduction. Best on the drawing board and best behind the wheel are two widely separated things."

1959

JULY 1959 ▼

Silver Hawk—Studebaker's Agile Sportscar/Coupe

Studebaker was already fading, and to eyes soon to see the twenty-first century, the 180-horsepower V-8 Silver Hawk looked anything but simple, but that's how *MT's* Chuck Nerpel saw it.

"Somewhere in the vast collection of horsepower, garish chrome, extra-long wheelbase, excessive overhang, bulging widths, interiors by ultra-modern decorators, and instrument panels by Salvador Dali, there must be a domestic automobile that is a simple, functional vehicle. We think we found the answer in Studebaker's Silver Hawk sport coupe. Here is a compact package with enough front seat width to accommodate the driver and two passengers, and a back seat for those occasional extra riders. Although legroom is surprisingly good, the body shape is still that of a two-door coupe, and not a long sedan with two doors eliminated."

1963 Corvette Sting Ray Coupe

"Sting Ray" nomenclature debuted on the Corvette in '63, and what a grand entry it proved to be. new from the ground up, the third-generation Vette continued with its well-engiineered arsenal of powerful V-8s, but added independent rear suspension and a striking new Bill Mitchell-penned body with hideaway headlamps and elegantly sculpted lines. The back glass on the racy fastback coupe model was split by a central pillar.

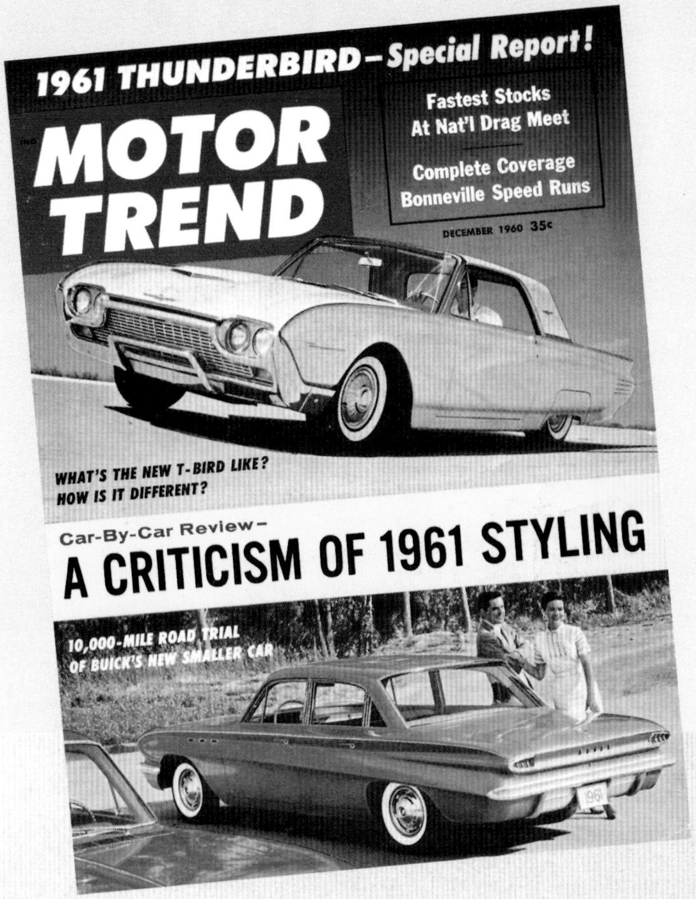

2

The 1960s

1960–1969

There is no one perfect explanation for the '60s. Among the tumult were the truly oppressed justly gaining their rights and the self-indulgent pushing the limits of acceptable behavior. There were scientific breakthroughs by the bushel and a widespread, enthusiastic embrace of bizarre mysticism. The country came together to put a man on the moon and was

FEBRUARY 1964

1964 Thunderbird Road Test

Ford's T-Bird entered its fourth generation in '64 with new sharp-edged styling, and a 300-horsepower 390-cubic inch V-8 under its hood. MT drove a hardtop, but the convertible and sport roadster also continued to be available.

"One additional item that should accompany milady when she drives her Thunderbird downtown for a shopping spree is an Auto Club membership. Should a tire go flat, few women would be able to wrestle the heavy spare wheel and tire out of its high resting place or over the trunk's high lip. Ford's Thunderbird fills its intended purpose. It's a real prestige four-seater. Granted it's not everyone's cup of tea, but for bird-lovers, it's the 'only way to fly.' Flight plans, anyone?"

JANUARY 1960 ▲

Corvair Road Test

Chevrolet's Corvair, with its rear-mounted air-cooled flat-six engine and all-independent suspension, was radically different from any other domestic car. As impressive as the Corvair's engineering was (enough for *Motor Trend* to make it '60s Car of the Year), the swing axle rear suspension proved its undoing. That suspension is what made the car notoriously skittish and led to Ralph Nader's 1966 book *Unsafe at Any Speed*, devastating the Corvair (which had been redesigned for '65) and inspiring a flood of automotive safety regulations.

"Cornering on sharp switchbacks is not for the Corvair. Because of the necessity to decrease oversteer of swing axles for the average driver, the rearend geometry assumes extreme lean. While this lean is slight, it does cause the rear wheels to judder as they attempt to follow a slip angle line and steering line that are just too far apart."

ripped apart by war in Vietnam and a slew of political assassinations. It was a decade of sexual liberation and psychedelia, and the decade that elected Richard Nixon to the presidency.

The forces that affected society during the '60s, of course, affected the auto industry. Foremost among those was the rise of the Baby Boomer generation born after World War II, a generation not devoted to Detroit's products, as were their parents, and demanding more choices.

Volkswagen may have only sold two Beetles during 1949 in the United States, but it sold 120,442 during '59. That got Detroit's attention. America's initial response to the imports was the '60 Chevrolet Corvair, Ford Falcon, and Plymouth Valiant compacts. While the Falcon and Valiant were essentially scaled-down versions of traditional Detroit iron, the Corvair dared to be more import-like with its rear-mounted, air-cooled flat-six engine and all-independent suspension. It was the uniqueness of the Corvair that would eventually make it—arguably—the most important car of the '60s.

The compacts were an instant hit; in 1960, Ford sold 435,676 Falcons; Chevy sold 250,007 Corvairs; and Plymouth shipped 192,364 Valiants. But those sales didn't come at the expense of VW, which saw its own sales rise to 159,995 cars during the same year, and makers ranging from Alfa Romeo to Toyota and Volvo also were experiencing growth in the United States.

On the heels of the compacts, Detroit introduced a series of "intermediates" that split the difference between the full-size and compact lines. For '62, Ford introduced the Fairlane, and Chrysler massaged its Dodge Dart and Plymouth Fury models so they were smaller than the Dodge 880 and big Chryslers. GM's A-body family of intermediates appeared in '64 with the Chevrolet Chevelle, Oldsmobile Cutlass, and Buick Special. Still these were all merely prelude to the two definitive youth-oriented vehicles of the '60s, both of which debuted in '64. Those cars were, of course, Ford's Mustang and Pontiac's powerful GTO.

That first Mustang wasn't much more than a Falcon with a sleeker, sexier body. But it was sexy and it was affordable (barely more than a Falcon), and that made it a sensation. The Mustang was introduced April 17, 1964, and in just four months, 100,000 of them were sold. And during '65, Ford put over 550,000 people in Mustang coupes, convertibles, and fastbacks. What the car lacked in daring engineering, it made up for in youthful spirit; it defiantly wasn't a car any baby boomer's parents had driven.

The Mustang defined a new class of car: the ponycar. By '67, Chevy had its version in the Camaro, Pontiac had the Firebird, Plymouth the Barracuda, and by '68, AMC brought forth the Javelin.

The Mustang could initially be had with a 170-cubic inch I-6 making 101 horsepower or a 164-horsepower 260-cubic inch V-8. Only later would performance build the car's legendary status. On the other hand, the Pontiac GTO's key element was speed. With up to 348 horsepower on tap when its 389-cubic inch V-8 wore the famous "Tri-Power" three two-barrel carburetors, the GTO may have looked like a regular Tempest Le Mans two-door, but it went like a Ferrari. It was the first of the musclecars, a genre that would define the rest of the decade.

While Detroit was pushing forward with its products, the imports were steadily gaining momentum in the United States. BMW refined the "Sport Sedan" during this period, Mercedes-Benz defined a new European style of luxury, VW continued to grow, and Japanese makers like Toyota and Datsun produced cars that would begin to attract buyers on merits other than price.

Pushing to get young people interested in their products naturally led manufacturers to the racetrack. During the '60s, Ford was active in NASCAR, drag racing, and, most notoriously, endurance racing where Ford took on Ferrari and won. Chrysler brought back the Hemi in '66 to go stock car racing, and in '67, Richard Petty used that engine to race to the most successful season in NASCAR history. He drove to 27 victories that year, including 10 straight. The legend Petty built makes Chrysler's Hemi-powered street cars among the most collectible and valuable muscle machinery ever. GM's racing efforts led to cars like the '67 Z28 Camaro optimized for competition in the SCCA's Trans-Am road racing series, as well as the awe-inspiring '69 ZL-1 Corvette with its all-aluminum 427 swiped from the world-beating McLaren Can-Am racers.

But the automotive event of the '60s wouldn't take place on a racetrack, but in America's bookstores. In '66 a young Washington, D.C., lawyer, Ralph Nader, published his book, *Unsafe At Any Speed*, which used the Chevy Corvair to indict the entire auto industry for its woeful lack of concern about safety. It ignited a firestorm of public outrage, which translated into political action and wound up in legislation—a steady stream of government regulations defining how cars should and would be built. Ultimately the country emerged from the '60s with a new and continuing consumer movement and an emerging radical expansion of both public interest and private interest product liability lawsuits. The automotive world hasn't been the same since.

As suspicious as many Americans had become about automotive safety and the effect of the automobile on the environment, the country still loved cars as the decade ended. After all, the number-one movie of 1969 was the story of a Volkswagen with a soul: Disney's *The Love Bug.*

JULY 1960 ▸

Tomorrow's Corvette?

Stories about the future of the Corvette are a mainstay of every car magazine. In 1959 and 1960, Chevy showed the XP-700 which was based on a standard '58 Corvette chassis and was powered by a fuel-injected V-8. The car began life as a personal car for GM's chief stylist Bill Mitchell and featured tail styling that would transfer, nearly intact, to the production '61 Vette.

"Chief General Motors Stylist William L. Mitchell takes credit for the car's design, but he has been influenced, however subtly, by customizers. Witness the floating grille—a technique developed over the years by MT Custom Car Editor George Barris. Also, the clear glass headlights resemble Lucas driving lights—much in favor by Barris in his recent customs."

When doing any sort of driving [the tach] is difficult to read, and on winding mountain roads where the Impala SS will be a marvelous car to drive, the wheel spoke will obscure it entirely from view.

—"Chevy's Hot 409"
June 1961

SEPTEMBER 1961 ▲

Corvette: Full Range Road Test

The Corvette is likely the most tested car in *Motor Trend's* history. To sample the full Corvette experience, the magazine tested two examples both running four-speed manual transmissions and powered by 283-cubic inch V-8s: one with a four-barrel carburetor rated at 230 horsepower and the other packing the 315-horse fuel-injected version. One was the mildest Corvette then available, the other the hottest.

"A good comparison of the performance potential of the two cars cannot be gained by merely comparing their low-speed and mid-range performance figures, because there really isn't a large numerical difference. However a time of 8.3 seconds 0-60 mph for the mild engine as compared to 7.4 seconds for the hot version will impress those who have experience in the field of acceleration testing."

MAY 1961 ▲

Thunderbird: A Real Change . . . For the Better

Always Ford's glamour car, the Thunderbird entered its third generation with new bullet-like styling and significantly more luxury. It also got a new 390-cubic inch V-8 rated at 300 horsepower. But at around 2 tons, the coupe and convertible were also the heaviest 'Birds yet; 0-60 mph took a full 10.5 seconds.

"Inadequate provision for luggage is the new Thunderbird's only serious fault and is a natural consequence of one of the car's greatest overall virtues, small overall size. The idea of a luxurious, sophisticated design on a short wheelbase remains exclusive with Ford."

MAY 1961 ▲

First Report: XK-E

The most beautiful car of the '60s? Many would say it was Jaguar's XK-E open roadster and coupe. Unique, gorgeous, and with a 3.8-liter/265-horsepower twin-cam six under its hood, the E-Type remains an icon of Jaguar, Britain, and pure sex appeal.

"The influence of the D-Type competition Jaguar is evident in the sleek lines of the XK-E roadster. The all-steel body features semi-unit construction with special sub-framing for the engine and springs."

Avanti, freely translated from Italian means "forward!", which is just where Studebaker's president Sherwood Egbert hopes to lead his company with an exciting new 1963 automobile.

—*"Motor Trend Road Test, Avanti" July 1962*

APRIL 1962 ▶

MT Road Test: Europe's Luxury Cars

At the upper end of automotive existence in '62 sat the Rolls-Royce Silver Cloud II, Mercedes-Benz 300, and Facel Vega Excellence.

"As everyone knows, the Rolls does not come cheaply. Suggested base price of the Silver Cloud II, $15,655, makes it the most costly of the current luxury imports. While this price includes radio, heater, leather, and whitewalls, there are a number of extras often added. A typical list includes air conditioning at $795, electric antenna $72, electric windows $220, and a necessary evil, transportation, delivery, and handling of about $150 on the West Coast, bringing a total to $16,892—plus tax and license."

DECEMBER 1961 ▶

The All-New Triumph TR-4

Into the '60s, a sports car more often than not meant a British sports car. Triumph's TR-4, powered by a 2.1-liter/100-horsepower OHV four was state of the art in '62. *"The ride is more comfortable than on the TR-3, and at the same time the car holds its course better on the straight and seems to have lost the peculiar tail-end twitch in the corners. In appearance, performance, passenger space, and luggage accommodations the TR-4 represents a big step forward—a civilized sports car in which one can travel fast in comfort."*

HOW STOCK IS STOCK? - 1963 NASCAR Modification and Safety Rules

IND MOTOR TREND

MARCH 1963 50¢ IN CANADA 60¢

MERCURY GOES RACING

FORD'S SECRET RACING V-8?

ROAD TESTS:

JEEP Becomes a Gentleman

PONTIAC'S '421' Family Car

CHEVROLET IMPALA

MERCURY Notchback Sedan

PETERSEN PUBLISHING COMPANY

Perhaps Ford Engineering has the engine hidden away in their own laboratories. For several years, there have been scattered rumors leaking out of Dearborn about a small aluminum V-8 in Ford's research section . . . Whether this is actually the engine Ford plans to use in their 1963 Indy car is still debatable.

—"Does Ford Have a Secret Racing Engine?"
March 1963

1963

APRIL 1963

MT Road Test: Buick Riviera

Perhaps the most beautiful American car of the '60s was Buick's sophisticated Riviera coupe. With a 340-horsepower 425-cubic inch V-8 under its hood, the Riviera was athletic (it went 0-60 in just 8.1 seconds) and luxurious, an intoxicating combination in such a big car. Buick would keep the Riviera in its line until '98.

"It's interesting to note that, without the added weight of test equipment and passenger, the Riviera's capable of cutting 0-60 mph in less than eight seconds. The engine is so smooth around town that you never get a hint of how exceptional the acceleration really is in this car."

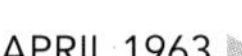

APRIL 1963

Motor Trend's Riverside 500

Motor Trend's commitment to motorsport expanded in 1963 when it became the title sponsor of the NASCAR Riverside 500 on Southern California's Riverside Raceway road course. In only his third NASCAR race, the winner was the legendary California road racer Dan Gurney. A.J. Foyt, who also then-rarely ran in NASCAR competition, finished second. Amazingly, Gurney would win the race again in '64, '65, and '66. The race became the "*Motor Trend* 500" in '64 and the magazine's sponsorship would remain in place through 1971. NASCAR racing continued at Riverside until '88, when the track closed to make room for a shopping mall.

"As the California sun sank slowly in the west, Dan Gurney sat on the roof of his 427-cubic-inch Ford and collected the beautiful Motor Trend *trophy from his wife and the Race Queen Margie McNally and, last but certainly not least, a check for $14,400 from Robert Petersen, promoter of the race and publisher of the magazine you're now reading."*

1963

MAY 1963 ▲

MT Road Test: Corvette

With its all-independent suspension, spectacular Sting Ray styling, and distinctive split rear window, the all-new '63 Corvette coupe was a sensation. *Motor Trend* tested the car powered by its most legendary powerplant, the fuel-injected 360-horsepower 327-cubic inch small-block V-8. Stirring the Muncie four-speed transmission furiously, *MT*'s drivers hustled the Vette 0-60 mph in just 5.8 seconds and completed the quarter-mile in 14.5 seconds at 102 mph.

"We thought the old model cornered darn well, but there's no comparing it to this new one. It does take a little different technique, but once the driver gets onto it, it's beautiful."

AUGUST 1963 ◀

MT Road Test: Volkswagen 1500 and 1200

Volkswagen moved to supplement its Beetle line in '63 with the addition of the 1500 sedan, which would eventually evolve into the familiar Fastback coupe and Squareback wagons. *MT* got an early chance to test the privately imported 1500 in direct comparison to the 1200 Beetle before the former went on sale here. *"The best conclusions we can draw from the two cars is that the 1200 will continue to keep its advocates happy. The reason for its continuing dominance of the import picture are sound, based on quality and long-range economy. When and if the 1500 appears on the scene here, it, too, should find success. Our own informal and highly incomplete survey of current VW owners revealed an interest in stepping up to the 1500. Both cars are sure to keep the import pot boiling for years to come."*

SEPTEMBER 1963 ▶

MT Road Test: Ford-Shelby-AC-Cobra

No man in automotive history has had more tall tales accumulate around him than Carroll Shelby. And most are about his stunning Cobras; A.C. Bristol sports cars overstuffed with Ford 289- and, eventually, 427-cubic inch V-8s. *Motor Trend* got its first taste of Shelby's alchemy when it drove this 271-horsepower 289-equipped Cobra. *"During our quarter-mile acceleration runs, we were bothered by excessive wheelspin in first gear that, with more rubber on the rear, our 0-60-mph times could've dropped 5.8 seconds down to around 5 flat. The 0-30- and 0-45-mph marks would also be correspondingly lower. We were very pleased with the quarter-mile averages (104 mph, 13.8-second e.t.), even though this isn't quite so fast as the near-13-second-flat, 112- to 114-mph figures that have been quoted elsewhere. But our test car wasn't a specially prepared prototype—just a well-used demonstrator. Top speed was also shy of the advertised mark of 150 mph. At 5800 rpm in fourth gear (actual 130 mph), the Cobra was just about through. A stretch any longer than the Riverside Raceway backstretch would have allowed another to 5 miles an hour."*

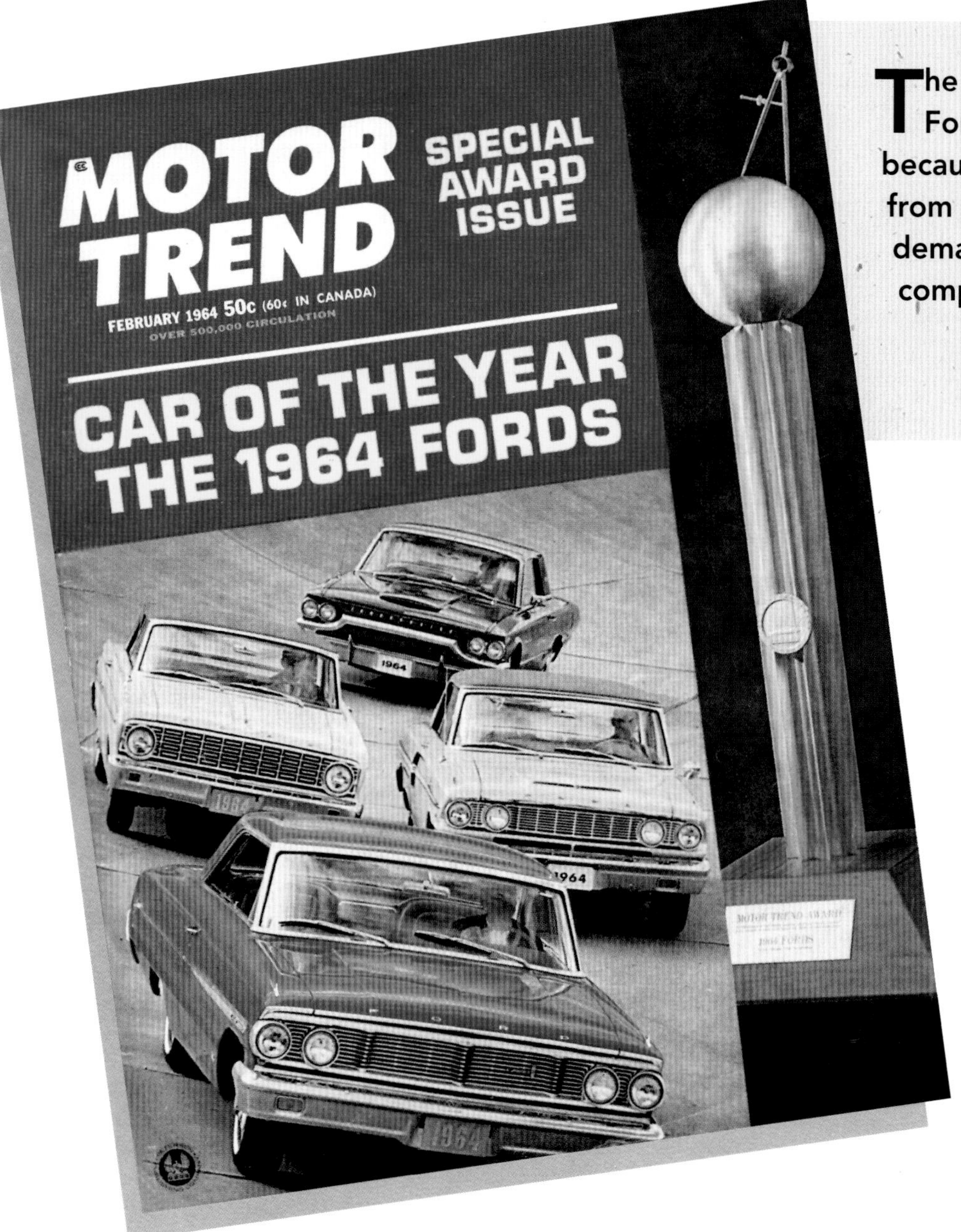

The editors of *Motor Trend* believe the 1964 Fords offer a better product to the public because of engineering improvements evolved from testing under the most rugged and demanding conditions ever conceived—open competition.

—*"Car of the Year" February 1964*

JANUARY 1964

Mercedes-Benz 300SE Road Test

No car had a more commanding road presence than the beautiful 300SE convertible. Even 35 years after its introduction the car retains its elegance and style.

"No car is perfect, but the Mercedes comes as close as any car can. Even the 300SE has room for improvement, and our suggestions are just that—suggestions. For our money, we feel the car should have power seats and windows. No automobile can be all things to all men, but Mercedes tries, and comes very close. Now, if they could only get the price down a bit."

JANUARY 1964 ▲

Tempest GTO Road Test

Stealing its name from a world champion Ferrari, Pontiac's GTO may not have been the first musclecar, but it was the car for which the term musclecar was invented. It was essentially a Tempest with a big 389-cubic inch engine under its hood and enough attitude to intimidate any other midsize car on any boulevard. How quick was that first GTO? The four-speed 325-horsepower convertible tested ran 0-60 mph in 7.7 seconds and dusted the quarter mile in 15.8 seconds at 93 mph. And, yes, wheelspin was a major limiting factor.

"The '389' engine isn't the only thing that makes a Tempest into a GTO. Pontiac has wisely made this a complete performance package by including such goodies as stiffer suspension with specially valved shock absorbers, a seven-blade 18-inch fan complete with cut-off switch, dual exhaust system, special 14-inch wheels with six-inch-wide rims (fitted with red-stripe premium, nylon-cord, low-profile tires), and a 10.4-inch Belleville clutch with gray-iron pressure plate for gearshift cars. In addition to all this, special trim and identification medallions tell onlookers this is a 'GTO 6.5-liter' automobile. Twin (fake) airscoops adorn the hood of the GTO and are found on no other Tempest model."

MAY 1964

Daytona 500

Richard Petty won his first Daytona 500 in 1964 behind the wheel of a Plymouth with Chrysler's fabulous hemispherical head 426-cubic inch V-8 engine under its hood. The engine was incredibly successful on the track, pushing lap speeds above 170 mph at Daytona for the first time, and resulting in a 1-2-3 Plymouth sweep. But the NASCAR Hemi was also essentially undrivable on the street and practically unavailable. It wasn't until 1966 that a "street" Hemi could be ordered. Petty went on to win the championship in 1964, but rule changes to tame the Hemi engine in 1965 resulted in a boycott by Chrysler for most of that season.

"Following his ever-so-simple victory, winner Petty commented that, 'unless Ford comes up with something new, I don't see why there should be much difference in the rest of the races this year.' "

MAY 1964

Barracuda!

Every Chrysler fanatic is convinced that the first true "ponycar" was, in fact, a fish. Plymouth's fastback version of the Valiant compact, the Barracuda, appeared in showrooms just before the Mustang did. Others, however, point out that the 'Cuda didn't go on sale until May and was merely a Valiant with a swoopy tail rather than a unique model itself.

"The Barracuda's fastback styling should make it even faster than the standard Valiant, which is quite a performer, while its four-passenger capacity makes it a natural for the sports-car-loving family with children. It's not often you can have your cake and eat it, too, but the combination of sport styling and the Valiant's proven good handling and performance should make the Barracuda a very desirable automobile."

AUGUST 1964 ▲

Mustang Road Test

Reviewing the '64 automotive year without mentioning the Mustang would be like describing breathing without referring to inhaling. The Mustang's April 17 debut was bigger than any movie opening, and the youth marketing success of the decade. It forged a whole new youth-oriented segment of the market for cars, and refocused advertising of almost all products as appeals to the young. *Motor Trend* first tested a Mustang coupe powered by the top-of-the-line 271-horsepower, 289-cubic inch V-8 and four-speed manual transmission. It bounded to 60 mph in just 7.5 seconds and knocked out the quarter-mile in 15.7 seconds at 89 mph.

"Few test cars have given us more sheer pleasure per mile than our bright poppy-red Mustang without wheel covers (they hadn't been made for the 15-inch wheels yet). And for the selling price of $3361.45 in Los Angeles, it gives a high performance-per-dollar value. Just listening to that engine is enough to send an enthusiast into a glassy-eyed trance."

Pontiac used to use the phrase Chief of the Sixes to plug its six-cylinder cars. Its latest Wild Indian with the powerful ohc medicine should bring this tribe back into prominence like nothing ever has.

—*"Tempest's New Cammer!"*
September 1965

JUNE 1965 ▲

Uncorking the Coronet '426'

All of Chrysler seemed obsessed with racing in the mid-'60s. The Coronet 500 with the 365-horsepower 426 "Wedge" head V-8 was exactly the right car, not for NASCAR stock car racing, but campaigning in the NHRA's stock classes where teams like the famous Ramchargers racked up wins regularly. But this car looked so boring. It was the proverbial sleeper that rocketed to 60 in just 7.7 seconds and knocked out a 15.7-second e.t. in the quarter-mile with an 89-mile-per-hour trap speed. That's despite a set of thin and greasy 8.25x4 whitewall tires.

"From a traffic light or when passing on the freeway, a heavy foot, well applied, would open all four throats on the AFB-3859S Carter carb. Then things really began to happen. Simultaneously, we were smashed back into Dodge's comfortable front buckets, the tach needle headed for 5500 rpm, and the speedometer needle dove toward the far end of its scale. To speak modestly, acceleration was impressive and certainly all anyone who drives on public roadways can handle."

MAY 1965 ▶

Shelby GT350

Moments after the Mustang fastbacks appeared, Carroll Shelby was gutting them to build his GT350. With a modified 289 V-8, beefed suspension, arrogant side-exit exhausts, and shorn of its back seat, the GT350 was first and foremost a race car licensed for the street. Shelby built 562 GT350s in '65, and 35 of those became GT350 R-Models for competition. But for a race car, the 306-horsepower 289-cubic inch V-8-powered "regular" GT350 was a fabulous street machine.

"When you start the engine, you're first impressed with a raucous note from the twin exhausts. These emerge just in front of each rear wheel. They're actually louder inside the car, because there's no insulation or undercoating. Handling is much improved over even the handling-kit-equipped normal Mustang. The GT350's best handling quality won't show with half-hearted cornering, though. You have to corner hard enough to take all the slack out of the suspension in one direction.

FEBRUARY 1965

Ford Makes a Tiger of the Sunbeam

Carroll Shelby wasn't the only one who thought that Ford V-8s deserved to be in tiny sports cars. With a 164-horsepower 260-cubic inch V-8 shoehorned in, the mild Sunbeam Alpine became the ravenous Tiger.

"With a comfortable, roomy interior, fully instrumented dash, and outstanding performance, the Tiger's a lot of sports car for $3499. That's about as much fun as anyone can buy for the price."

We road-tested the first production Charger and in eyeing it from every angle, nowhere could we find evidence of that compromise so evident in some of the other recently introduced fastbacks.

—*"Dodge's Charging Charger"*
January 1966

MAY 1966 ▶

Whither AMC?

American Motors was always in trouble. Cobbled together from the remnants of Nash-Kelvinator, Willys-Overland, and Hudson, AMC's existence was always threatened and never less than precarious. The rumble-seated '66 prototype seen here would eventually evolve into the production '68 Javelin and AMX sport coupes.

"Eventually, AMC has to achieve solidity, distinctiveness—and most important—uniqueness. It is not large enough to combat the Big Three on their terms. It must find its own individual product offering, one that sets it apart from its big brethren, yet embodies enough appeal to attract at least 500,000 customers annually."

1966

SEPTEMBER 1966 ▲

Road Test: Cobra 427

Many cars are beloved, but few are intimidating. And of those that are intimidating, none was more so than the monstrously powerful Shelby Cobra 427. In place of the 289-cubic inch small block Ford V-8 installed in the first Cobras, Shelby inserted Ford's NASCAR-spec 425-horsepower, 427-cubic-inch big-block monster into the basic AC shell. However it wasn't merely an engine swap; the chassis and suspension were also redesigned to handle the massive powerplant and its accompanying torrent of power. The 5.3-second 0-60-mile-per-hour performance (and 13.8 second at 106 mph quarter-mile clocking) recorded by *Motor Trend* was bettered in other tests in better broken-in Cobras wearing wider tires.

"Assuming you have the money, if you want a car that will cruise effortlessly at high speed and will always give you the feeling that you are driving it, you can't do better. If you want to pretend that every stoplight is the grid at Nurburgring or every freeway the Mulsanne straight, forget it. You can't afford the tickets."

JUNE 1966

Road Test: Citroën DS-21

In an automotive world of conventional engineering assumptions, Citroën's aerodynamic DS-21 was defiantly eccentric. In place of springs, it had a self-leveling hydropneumatic suspension. It was among the first cars to run on mandatory radial tires, and in place of a brake pedal, the car used a button on the floor. And, of course, it was a front-driver long before front drive captured the rest of the world. Power came from a hemi-headed four making 109 horsepower, which was good enough to push the compact-outside, huge-inside, 2,860-pound car to 60 mph in 12.8 seconds.

"The Citroën ride, derived from its self-leveling hydropneumatic suspension system, can only be compared to that of an airliner hitting isolated pockets of gentle to moderate turbulence. You go up or down, but by then, the leveling system is in action so there is no feeling of sudden return to normal and thus, no shock. In extreme dips, we could bottom the car at the front end, but the rear never did and there was no rebound whatever."

SEPTEMBER 1966

24 Hours to End Them All—Le Mans

After failing to buy Ferrari in 1963, Ford became determined to beat the Italian manufacturer at its own game: endurance racing. The result was the legendary GT40 sports car program that produced thrilling mid-engine sports prototypes powered by engines taken straight out of NASCAR stock cars. In 1966, Ford's ambitions for the program came to full fruition at Le Mans, where GT40 Mark IIs finished one-two-three and arrogantly strove to stage a "dead-heat" finish.

"It was impossible to find out where and by whom the decision had been made to rig a dead-heat finish. Out in the pits, they were saying that Ford management wanted (Ken) Miles, (Bruce) McLaren, and (Ronnie) Bucknam, if possible, all to cross the line abreast because it would make such a useful picture."

The two cars are apart yet fairly close. Shelby-American built the GT 500 with the idea of getting more customers for street-type vehicles than they could with the race-oriented GT 350s of the past. Oddly enough, this is what Chevrolet's theory has been too.

—*"Road Test: Shelby GT 500 & 427 Sting Ray"*
April 1967

JANUARY 1967

Road Test: Eldorado Switches from Push to Pull

Using components from the Oldsmobile Toronado, Cadillac revived the Eldorado for '67 with front drive under a spectacularly angular body. Power came from a 340-horsepower 429-cubic inch V-8 and, despite weighing in at over 4,700 pounds, the gigantic two-door reached 60 mph in 8.9 seconds.

"Shrewd work with sheetmetal has created a car that is instantly recognizeable as a Cadillac with hardly an impression of the other cars that share the same body shell. Eschewing the curves of the Toronado, Eldorado features crisp, tailored, almost razor-sharp lines. Prominent identification mark is the coffin-shaped hump on the hood, which was likened to the Cord by more than one onlooker, and, incidentally, the Eldorado was a real attention-getter. Styling of any car may be a question of taste, but Cadillac has done a fine job with the trick task of mating a classic, elegant look to contemporary verve. It's come quite a way in good taste since the garish fins of the late '50s."

MAY 1967 ▲

Sporty Specialties: Mustang, Camaro, and Barracuda

Motor Trend got a feel for the V-8 range of the new '67 Chevrolet Camaro in a comparison with Ford's Mustang and Plymouth's Barracuda (both of which were redesigned for '67). The three Camaros evaluated were a Z28 coupe powered by the racing-intended 302-cubic inch V-8 underrated at 290 horsepower, an RS/SS convertible carrying the 325-horse 350 and a two-speed Powerglide automatic, and an RS/SS coupe with the bruising 325-horsepower 396 big block under its hood. The quickest proved to be the big block car, which ripped to 60 mph in just 6.0 seconds, while the convertible performed the same feat in 6.8 seconds, and the high-revving Z28 needed a full 7.0 seconds to hit a mile a minute. However, though the Z28 got to 60 last, its 96-mile-per-hour trap speed at the end of the quarter-mile was the highest and indicative of its upper-end push that's perfect for racing.

"A handling-packaged Camaro feels the best on tighter turns because it understeers less than the others. The convertible model of the Camaro, because of the several hundred extra pounds weight, has a tendency to bottom on its suspension when going over dips more so than the other cars."

FEBRUARY 1967 ▲

Racing's Elusive Pot of Gold

Road racing has always been a tough sell in the United States. But if any series came close to the major leagues of American motorsport, it was the old Canadian-American Challenge Cup Series (the Can-Am). Inaugurated in 1966, the series brought together legendary race car builders and the guttural roar of large-displacement American V-8s to produce some of the most radical race cars of all time. The rules left cars to run virtually unlimited engines making over 600 horsepower. By the time the series faded in the early '70s, the turbocharged Porsche 917-30 had raised that horsepower mark to well over 1,000. They were the orange McLarens with big Chevy engines and drivers like Dennis Hulme and Bruce McLaren himself that dominated the early Can-Am. But even they had a hard time making the series pay.

"McLaren's team manager and partner E.E. (Teddy) Mayer categorized costs into five groups (for a race weekend): transportation ($10,950) involving round-trip freight and air fare charges for cars and personnel, and such items as tow trucks and car rental; per diem expenses ($7875), seven people at $15 per day; wages and fees ($17,300), four mechanics, team manager and drivers at $500 per race; depreciation of equipment ($7350), pro-rated over a full season; and miscellaneous expenses ($2200)—for a grand total of $45,675."

Anthony Granatelli was miles . . . away by now and when he spoke it was very soft. 'It will never be over . . . never . . .'

—*"Loser of the Year"*
May 1968

NOVEMBER 1968 ▸

Road Testing the Twilight Zone

In 1968, no cars were more exotic than the $15,750 Ferrari 330 GTC (front), $15,750 Lamborghini 400 2+2 (left), $18,900 Maserati Ghibli (center), or $17,200 Aston Martin DBS (right).

"Forget about the Jaguar XK-E and those Mercedes 280SLs and Porsche 911s. They only cost maybe $6000-8000 and that's for the proles. Almost everybody has them; you can even go to the bank and borrow money to buy one. Forget about those Rolls-Royces and Bentleys and the rest of that stuff, too. They got like, well, they got four doors and all that. They have an image, but it's not what you're looking for. If it is, turn the page and read about the new Dodge or how you can get a Turbo-HydraMatic on practically all the Chevys or some other example of what the Great Technology, vintage '69, hath wrought."

JANUARY 1968 ▲

Testing the Javelin

The ponycar ranks swelled in '68 with the addition of AMC's Javelin. The tested Javelin was powered by a 343-cubic inch four-barrel V-8 rated at 280 horsepower and backed by a four-speed manual transmission. That propelled the Javelin a 0-60-mile-per-hour time of 7.6 seconds and a 15.1-second at 93-mile-per-hour quarter-mile blast.

"American Motors is very sincere in their flattery. They've copied the other makers' basic sports-personal idea, but that's where the imitation ends. The Javelin is a world apart from the other ponycars in styling, comfort, space, and features. It also differs in the fact that never has one car meant so much to the corporate life of a company. For AM's sake, Javelin has to be a success."

Is it practical?
DIESEL POWER FOR YOUR CAR
MOTOR TREND
5 CAR TEST: Camaro, Mustang, Javelin, Firebird, Cougar
Personality: GM's Chief Stylist Bill Mitchell
GREAT MOMENTS AT NÜRBURGRING by Leo Levine
Import Test: DATSUN'S HOT ANSWER TO VW
50¢ MARCH, 1969
UK 4/3 Sweden KR. 3.95 Inkl. moms
NEW 302 MUSTANG Challenges Z-28 Camaro for sales and Trans-Am racing
REX MAYS 300 Dan Gurney wins at his track as Bobby Unser captures USAC Championship

We can see the kids now, all jammed down at their local dealer when the first Boss 302 hits the showroom. The dealer won't know what it is but the kids will.

—*"Boss 302"*
March 1969

APRIL 1969 ▸

Chevy Heads for the Hills

Amid all the muscle machinery of '69, Chevrolet introduced the Blazer, which, in retrospect, may have been the most important new vehicle introduction of the year. Not much more than a short pickup with an integral bed and a plastic camper shell that extended over the cab, the K-5 Blazer defined the American idea of the SUV. *"Success off the road is an admirable achievement for Detroit designers, because the thinking required is diametrically opposed to customary concepts. Where plastics and styling changes are primary in passenger cars, off-the-road vehicles must be virtually invulnerable. And where multiple model choices are offered in cars, simplicity is the foremost virtue off the road."*

MAY 1969 ▲

The ZL-1

In terms of pure performance, the '69 ZL-1 overwhelms every other Corvette. The heart of the ZL-1 was an all-aluminum 427-cubic inch big block with a 12.5:1 compression ratio and a high-rise/short-duration cam. Chevy claimed an unfathomable 585 horsepower at a towering 6,600 rpm for the engine, and it weighed 20-25 pounds less than a 350-horsepower 350 small block. *Motor Trend* drove the car, but was unable to test it.

"The ZL-1 has Ferrari speed plus Ferrari handling and Ferrari brakes, but without Ferrari fuss and bother so you can enjoy it. The ZL-1 doesn't just accelerate because the word accelerate is inadequate for this car. It tears its way through the air and across black pavement like all the modern big-inch racing machines you have ever seen.

PSSSST! SNEAK PREVIEW:
'70½ CAMARO and FIREBIRD
MOTOR TREND
Corvettes that didn't make it
$35,000 Volkswagen Limo
Balancing the Budget-
Duster vs Hornet vs
Maverick
JANUARY 1970 50¢
Dan Gurney goes to Plymouth-WHY?
The Ultimate Road Runner
SUPERBIRD!
Plymouth
1970
Exclusive! OUR BRONCO WINS BAJA 1000

3

The 1970s

1970–1979

The '70s were ugly. The clothes were ugly, the architecture ugly, the shag carpeting despicable, and the whole country seemed to take a decade-long wallow in economic malaise and spiritual dissatisfaction. And the cars? With notable exceptions, they were insufferable.

JUNE 1972

Sayonara Supercar

The names were familiar, but the cars were shadows of themselves when MT compared the Heavy Chevy, Ford Torino Gran Sport, Dodge Charger, and Pontiac GTO. The GTO and Charger (photo) were powered by a 300-horsepower, 455-cubic inch V-8 and a 240-horsepower, 340-cubic inch V-8, respectively. Not entirely slow, the GTO crunched on the quarter mile in 15.4 seconds at 92 mph, and the Charger did the same thing in 16.2 ticks at 89 mph.

"Unlike car companies, automotive insurers do not have a sense of humor. Sometimes, they appear to lack even a sense of common. Instead of growing concerned over what appeared to be a distressing trend, they hit the big red button and cranked out Supercar surcharges faster than a runaway Gatling gun. The decline, brought on by overkill in the horsepower department, was rapidly accelerated by surcharges. The Supercar has been mortally wounded. Mercifully, the government stepped in and put a bullet in the brain with more smog regulation."

FEBRUARY 1970 ▲

It's a Masserrariac, White Eyes

Both the Chevrolet Camaro and Pontiac Firebird entered 1970 freshly designed as second-generation GM F-Cars. Besides the voluptuous styling (hence *MT's* title for this story about the Firebird range), the new cars were more luxurious and more powerful. The star of the bunch? Likely the 370-horsepower 400-cubic inch Firebird Trans Am.

"The steering is exceptionally fast, perhaps too fast. At the limit, the gear ratio is 11:1—and that's getting down into go-kart country, brother. Combine this with the torque and low-speed response of the engine, and you've got a mandate that says, 'Be smooth or be gone—into the toolies.' "

Entering the decade, there seemed to be a general feeling that things couldn't continue the way they had with cars. Perhaps the most important single event indicating this was the passage of the Clean Air Act of 1970, which instituted a series of progressively more stringent emissions requirements on cars (and many other things).

Detroit, which had defined automotive aspiration as more power in more car, suddenly found itself unable to build any more power into vehicles. The height of the musclecar era was the '70 model year. By '71 reduced compression ratios lowered actual power outputs of the era's enormous engines. For example, the biggest engine of them all, the 500-cubic inch Cadillac V-8 used in the Eldorado, had a 10.0:1 compression ratio in 1970 and was rated at 400 horsepower by GM. In 1971, that same engine had 9.0:1 compression, and its maker rated it at 365 ponies. A switch from "gross" to SAE "net" horsepower ratings confuses the issue somewhat, but in the '75 model year, when catalytic converters became almost universal on North American-market new cars, that same Cadillac 500-incher's compression ratio had dropped to 8.5:1, and the power output was a claimed 190 horses. That's less than half what Cadillac had claimed just five years previously.

But while power outputs were dropping, at least initially, most cars were still getting bigger. Going back to the Cadillac example, the enormous '70 Eldorado weighed in at a portly

MARCH 1970 ▲

1970 Z/28: The Gray Deceiver

While the Trans Am was the star of Pontiac's new '70 1/2 Firebirds, the glory of Chevy's '70 1/2 Camaro was reserved for the Z/28. Dropping the specialized 302 V-8 used previously, the new Z/28 had the ample 350 cubic inch LT-1 V-8.

"The old engine was rated at 290 hp, the new one at 360. The old torque figure was 290 lbs.-ft., the new one 380 (at 4000 rpm). The whole thing is still built to run at high speeds, with extruded aluminum pistons, forged crank, and forged rods. We only ran it to 6000 rpm in top gear (119 mph with the standard 3.73:1 gearing and F60x15 tires), but it felt like it would go past the redline to 125 mph."

JUNE 1970 ▲

Motor Trend's 1970 Import Car of the Year: Porsche 914-914/6

In a year crammed with significant new sports cars like the Datsun 240Z, Porsche's innovative mid-engine 914 most impressed the staff, and it earned the magazine's top honor for import cars.

"Sure it was one of the best-handling machines any of us had ever driven, and no one faulted steering response or leg room, but the car underscores better than anything else the shift in automotive design influence out of America."

4,630 pounds. In '75, that half-as-powerful Eldo had swelled to gargantuan proportions and weighed in at a seriously obese 5,108 pounds. That's a 478-pound increase. No wonder cars were less fun to drive.

Half-hearted attempts by Detroit to build subcompact small cars resulted in vehicles like the '71 Chevrolet Vega and Ford Pinto. Essentially scaled-down big cars, they weren't without their technological innovations; the Vega had an all-aluminum overhead cam engine and the Pinto was the first U.S.-built vehicle with rack-and-pinion steering, for instance. But ultimately, the Vega's engine proved troublesome and the rest of the car poorly built. And the Pinto wound up a symbol for corporate indifference when its vulnerability to fires was uncovered in a series of lawsuits.

The absurdity of Detroit's almost pathological determination to continue business as usual in the '70s was made obvious during the 1973 OPEC oil embargo, which cut off the flow of imported oil into the United States. The result was rapidly rising gas prices and, even more dramatically, fuel shortages. Just try pushing a 5,000-pound bone-dry Cadillac up to the pump of the Mobil dealer and finding, after a two-hour wait, that you were only allowed to buy two or three gallons of gas. That's the sort of frustration that'll have you shopping for a Honda in no time.

And shopping for a Honda is just what a lot of Americans did. By the early '70s, the stigma of Japanese cars being "cheaply made tin boxes" was already fading on the strength of such attractive products as the '70 Datsun 240Z sports car, Toyota's ruggedly built Corolla, and an unceasing stream of outstanding consumer electronics from companies like Sony, Toshiba, and Panasonic. Amid the first fuel crisis, Honda announced its new Civic and despite its diminutive size, it immediately earned cachet as a "smart buy," while traditional Detroit iron was often dismissed as being "dinosaurish." By the end of the decade, many observers would argue that Japan's reputation for quality products easily outstripped that of America.

It may have been slow to respond, but eventually Detroit began to change its ways. Evidence of that came in cars like GM's "downsized" line of '77 full-size cars, which packed as much room as the superseded land yachts into cars that were, in the case of the Buick LeSabre, 10 inches shorter and almost a full half-ton lighter. It was also seen in the adoption of such technologies as electronic fuel injection on the '76 Cadillac Seville and turbocharging on Buick's 3.8-liter V-6 in '78. There

MAY 1970 ▲

"Isn't There an Easier Way to Earn My Canadian Club?"

Motor Trend's indulgence of obscure article titles peaked with A.B. Shuman's test of the '70 Plymouth 340, 440 Six-Pack, and 426 Hemi 'Cudas. To many Chrysler fanatics, the 425-horsepower '70 Hemi 'Cuda is the ultimate Mopar. And to those who've actually driven them, the 390-horsepower 440 Six-Pack is revered as one of the musclecars that best mixed great power with excellent manners (even though *MT* reviewer A.B. Shuman's experience was different). Even the far more common 275-horsepower 'Cuda 340 is collectable today.

"The (340's) ratchet shifter worked very well, allowing positive gear changes without danger of overshifting. Best run was 96 mph, with a 14.5 elapsed time. (The 440's) best was a 14.4 at 100 mph, just 0.1 second quicker than the 340 with a lot more work involved. The Hemi had to be babied 'til it was well on its way down the strip, as it could really spin the tires. Shifts were made at 6200 rpm, and the car was very consistent, 14.0s at 102 mph."

was also a brief flirtation with diesel power, which faded rapidly with poor sales and miserable reliability from gas engines converted to diesel operation.

As the '70s ended, Japanese and European manufacturers were no longer merely peripheral niche players in the American market, but mainstream alternatives to the Big Three. The Honda Accord, introduced in '76, was redefining the family car, while prestige for many now meant cars like the Mercedes 450SEL and BMW 733i, rather than the Cadillac DeVille or Lincoln Town Car. And high performance meant the Porsche 911 Turbo or Lamborghini Countach rather than the era's emaciated Corvettes.

The Big Three itself was in danger of becoming a Big Two or even a Big One, as Chrysler and Ford endured severe financial strain at the end of the decade. What was likely the ultimate event of Detroit's experience of the '70s actually took place in 1980, when Lee Iacocca, Chrysler's newly named chairman of the board, testified before Congress in favor of the Loan Guarantee Act, which would secure loans to ensure the corporation's survival with the full backing of the U.S. government. In the '50s, who could've imagined the top executive at any of the Big Three, the embodiment of free enterprise and successful capitalism, petitioning for a government bail-out?

The 450SL has significance beyond its appeal as a desirable or prestigious two-seater touring car. Its new fuel-injected 4 1/2-liter V-8 has already (with air pump and catalytic converter) met the tough 1975 emissions standards in the lab.

—*"450SL: Sicherheit and Lauterkeit (Safety and Purity)"*
June 1971

SEPTEMBER 1971 ▶

The Real American Station Wagon Test

Big, full-size Sport Utility Vehicles weren't unknown before the '90s. Of the Chevy Suburban, Jeep Wagoneer, and International Travelall, only the Suburban survived into the last decade of the century to experience today's SUV boom. International Harvester, which pioneered the SUV business with its Scouts and Travelall models, built its last Travelall in '75 and left the light-truck business altogether in '80. It survives today as Navistar, building large trucks again under the International name.

"Except for the Wagoneer, these vehicles as a class stand up as a sound alternative to the normal station wagon. Especially in the case of International Harvester, they represent a different manufacturing philosophy than the Average American is accustomed to. Even the sales approach is different. They know you need a vehicle to do a job, and if they build the best one they can, the public will buy it."

SEPTEMBER 1971 ▲

Alfa Romeo

Alfa Romeo's GTV sport coupe, two-seat Spider convertible, and Berlina four-door sedan all shared the same 1,779-cubic centimeter DOHC four that used fuel injection to produce an impressive 130 horsepower. The Spider and Berlina offered gracious Italian manners and real sporting verve, but the Bertone-bodied GTV was something special indeed to *MT*'s John Lamm.

"I've fallen in love with about 10 cars in my life that I'd seriously consider selling my soul for. Unfortunately, all but two are over $10,000 and only one is under $5000. That's the Alfa GTV."

JULY 1971 ▲

Ferrari Dino 246 GT versus Porsche 911S

The mid-engine $13,500 Dino was Ferrari's lowest-priced car, and the $9,471 911S Porsche's most expensive. But both were powered by six-cylinder engines, the Ferrari by a 2.4-liter DOHC V-6 making 225 horsepower, and the Porsche an air-cooled, horizontally opposed, 2.2-liter OHC motor rated at 200 horsepower. Either car today is considered among the most desirable of their respective breeds. The Ferrari was quicker (0-60 mph in 6.1 seconds, as opposed to the Porsche's 7.3-second performance), although Editor Eric Dahlquist preferred the driving experience of the Porsche. But he couldn't deny the Ferrari's looks.

"Side-by-side with even the likes of a 911S, the Dino's visual impact is so forceful you almost don't see the other car for a moment. With curves and bulges and flares and scoops sweeping over the silhouette, the Pininfarina-designed 246 is seemingly the epitome of the contemporary automobile."

FEBRUARY 1971 ▲

Commonsense Roadrunner

The diminution of the musclecar was apparent in *MT's* appraisal of the all-new '71 Plymouth Road Runner. Testing the 300-horsepower 383-cubic inch version (0-60 in 6.7 seconds, the quarter in 14.8 at 94.5 mph), *MT* was startled to discover it was marginally quicker than a similarly equipped car with the 385-horsepower 440-cubic-incher capped by triple carbs (0-60 in 6.7 seconds, the quarter in 15.0 at 96.0 mph). Both had three-speed automatic transmissions.

"For those whose hearts beat in time with the air-sucking, fuel-gulping triple-carbureted 440 and don't believe our times, we must concede that the big-engined Runner was in less than peak condition. In fact, it was with great reluctance that the Plymouth P.R. man even let us have it without further medical attention. To be fair, I checked our times on a Charger 440, which had the same rearend ratio (4.10:1) and was driven by A.B. Shuman, our resident drag racer. His quarter-mile times were better, 14.74-97.3 mph, but the intermediate times were very close to the ones we got and again slower than the 383."

1972

Right now, right here in 1972 Nixon-conservative America, the public has just bought another piece of magic, lock, stock, and barrel—the Wankel engine. And in a slow news-year, the Wankel is what's happening.

—*"Wankel"*
November 1972

JANUARY 1972 ▲

MT Impression: BMW 2002tii

The BMW cult expanded with the Kugelfischer-injected 2002tii. Thanks to the fuel-injection system, the 2.0-liter OHC four produced an admirable 140 horsepower, and the car ripped to 60 mph in an impressive-for-a-small-engine 9.9 seconds. The tii was to the 2002 what the original GTO was to the Pontiac Tempest.

"On balance, five-speed or no, the tii is one of the benchmarks in sedan touring car design, superbly executed and disappointing in only a few minor ways. At the time we were there, the factory was deliberating on the tii's final U.S. sticker, somewhere said to be in the neighborhood of $4100, or around $400 more than the old 2002. Excellence doesn't come cheap."

JULY 1972 ▲

The 26-State Border to Border Ocean to Ocean Audissey

MT's John Christy and Chuck Koch drove an Audi 100LS in a four-corner adventure through the United States.

"You don't realize the steady rate of knots and neither do cruising police unless one is foolish enough to catch them up too quickly from behind."

FEBRUARY 1972

Friendly Hostility

Off-road racing came into its own during the early '70s with men such as Vic Hickey tuning the Chevy Blazer and Bill Stroppe wrenching on the Ford Bronco. Each brought a civilian-ready, slightly modified example of his favorite truck out to Indian Dunes recreation area for *MT* to sample.

"After a cursory examination of the Bronco, Hickey said, 'How hard was it to drop that 351 into the car, Bill?' Stroppe, wearing the proper frown as he inspected the Blazer, allowing how there was an abundance of chrome, 'You didn't used to do that, Vic.' To which Hickey replied with one of the day's few serious comments: 'Christ, Bill, when the government won't let you sell power, you gotta give the people something.' "

JANUARY 1972 ▲

A Back Door to Economy

Few people now harbor much nostalgic fondness for the Chevrolet Vega, Ford Pinto, or AMC Gremlin. In '72, *MT* compared the three hatchback versions of Detroit's first subcompacts and found distinct differences between the three. The Gremlin was quickest, running 18.3 seconds at 76 mph in the quarter-mile. The Pinto and Vega should be finishing their runs in early 2002.

"Power is really an optimistic term in reference to the three small engines. Gremlin comes off the strongest, since the 'X' model comes with the 258-six as the bottom offering. Vega has a slight edge over Pinto both in response and horsepower (90 to 86), as well as noise. Neither is quite a stormer, but both are more than adequate to the task if judicious use is made of the four-speed box."

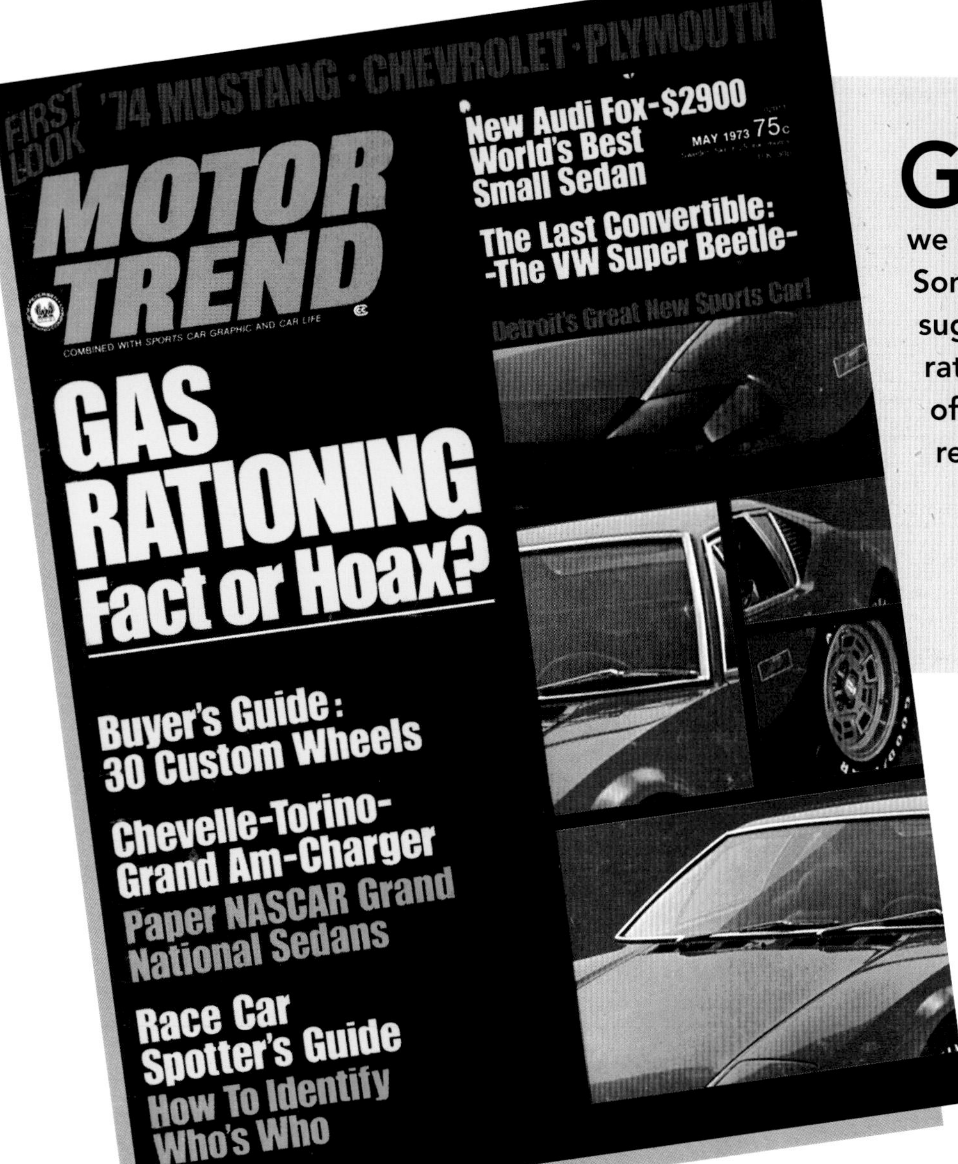

Gas rationing, if it ever comes, will be because the supply is short, not because we can't solve our smog problems. Somebody's got to be kidding when they suggest putting 7 to 9 million people on gas rationing. If they tried it, it might just touch off that revolution we've heard about in recent years.

—"Gas Rationing: Fact or Hoax?"
May 1973

SEPTEMBER 1973 ▲

Corvette versus Pantera

While the Corvette soldiered on into the early '70s, it faced new competition from the Italian-built, Ford-powered DeTomaso Pantera being sold through Lincoln-Mercury dealers. With 266 horsepower available from its 351-cubic inch V-8, the mid-engine '73 Pantera was a close match to the '73 Corvette's when equipped with the 275-horse 454-cubic inch V-8. "Father of the Corvette" Zora Arkus-Duntov attended the test at Ontario Motor Speedway. The Pantera lapped Ontario at 129.68 mph driven by MT's Eric Dahlquist, the production Corvette's best was 129.87 mph with Duntov behind the wheel, and the cheater car zipped around at 141.06 mph.

"Flat-Out Classic was not as conclusive as we would have liked. In the hands of mortals, the Pantera is the swifter in spite of a 103-cubic-inch and 9-horsepower deficit. In the hands of the master, it's the Corvette by the finest of margins."

SEPTEMBER 1973 ▲

Car of the Month: BMW's Fiery Turbo Car

By '73, BMW's reputation was solidly built on a succession of attractive sport sedans. The company had never offered the United States a sports car, however. It showed this mid-engine prototype (front) with gullwing doors and powered by a turbocharged version of the 2002tii's 2.0-liter four. The BMW Turbo would never go into production, but its shape would eventually evolve into the fabulous, six-cylinder-powered M1 introduced in late 1978.

"The Turbo is more than a correct projection, it is a preview peek into the product future of a group of people who know how to design and build some of the soundest and most exciting automobiles in Europe."

1974

LUCKY LICENSE BONUS . . . Details on Page 34
WIN THE 1974 CAR OF THE YEAR!
THE COMPLETE AUTOMOTIVE MAGAZINE
MOTOR TREND
COMBINED WITH SPORTS CAR GRAPHIC AND CAR LIFE
75¢ JANUARY 1974
END OF AN ERA
IS VOLKSWAGEN DUMPING THE BUG?
EXPOSÉ OF THE INTERLOCK SEATBELT
How it Works (and Doesn't)
ROTARY CORVETTE MODEL INSIDE
Final Exciting Chapter in the Secret Corvettes
HOW THE MID-SIZED WONDERS STACK UP
Matador-Charger-Malibu-Torino
DRIVING THE CHEAPEST AMERICAN CARS
Vega-Pinto-Gremlin-Colt Comparison
MR. FORD'S HANDS-DOWN CHAMP
8 Cars Elected to Hall of Fame
SCANDAL IN THE SOAP BOX DERBY
How Unc' Rigged the Race
MONTHLY DEPARTMENTS
AUTOPUZZLER!
NEW THIS MONTH
Question and Answer Quiz • Washington Listening Post
Competition • Classics and Antiques • Photo Quiz
Driveway Mechanic • Trendsetters • Recalls • Cycles
Recreational Vehicles • Pickups and Vans • High Performance

If there is any doubt that VW's one-car policy is dead, consider this: The 1974 VW model range includes nine versions of the Beetle, 25 variations of the newly born Dasher, 12 versions of the VW-412, and four versions of the VW K 70.

—"Is Volkswagen Dumping the Beetle?" January 1974

FEBRUARY 1974 ▶

Car of the Year: Ford Mustang II

From the view of the late '90s, the selection of the downsized, Pinto-based, four- and six-cylinder Mustang II as Car of the Year is ludicrous. But in the context of '74, it was obvious: a reinvention of the youth car for a time when fuel supplies were inconsistent and safety of more apparent concern to buyers than power. The market couldn't have reacted to the car more enthusiastically. Ford sold 134,817 of the big '73 Mustangs, and an unbelievable 385,993 smaller Mustang IIs in '74. *"Ten years ago, the first sport, performance-oriented but functional Mustang appeared. Those were different times, perhaps happier days. The Mustang then was most of all an 'alternative car'; the swoopy, full-size American car was both within the financial grasp of most Americans, and it was affordable to maintain and drive. Gas was almost half the price it is today, and there was plenty of it, and Ford engineers were not limited by power and economy-sapping anti-pollution devices. The free-wheeling, wide-open era of the American automobile, unfortunately, is over. Time to face reality."*

MAY 1974 ▶

Join 'Stop'! Help Save the Pantera

By the summer of '74, it was obvious that Ford was giving up on the mid-engine Pantera sports car. However they also tantalizingly leaked out this photo of the "Pantera 7X Safety Sports Car," which they hinted could be the '75 Pantera. *Motor Trend* swallowed the bait and printed a form so that readers could petition Ford to ensure the 7X made it to production. However, the car's Italian maker, DeTomaso, would continue building and developing the original Pantera into the '90s (and never again officially export it to the United States).

SEPTEMBER 1974 ▲

Car of the Month: The Silver Arrow III

GM's top stylist Bill Mitchell always had a particular passion for the Buick Riviera and built a few for his own use that indulged his sensibilities. The Silver Arrow III was based on the '71 Riv and forecast many features that were appearing on some '74 and '75 models and are common today.

"Starting at the front, the Silver Arrow III has six experimental recessed headlamps—nothing new today except, at the time it was built, rectangular headlamps were illegal. The rearview mirror has a built-in electric sensor, and when a car approaches from the rear at night with a high beam, the mirror automatically dims. Gas-tank readings are also electronic readouts, but instead of telling you that you're 'quarter full,' this one prints the number of gallons remaining in the 25-gallon tank. There's a digital clock, too."

1975

But what about this offensive 55-mph speed limit? The bad news is well known; it's here to stay. Both houses of Congress have perpetuated the lowered maximum speed indefinitely.

—*"Catch 55: The National Speed Limit"*
April 1975

DECEMBER 1975

What's a 150-mph Car Like You Doing in a 55-mph Country Like This?

In the face of 1975's grim realities of a new national 55-mile-per-hour speed limit and cars further asphyxiated by anti-pollution devices, Porsche announced the fabulous 911 Turbo. That first Turbo had only a four-speed transmission, but its 3.0-liter OHC flat-six was boosted to a fat 234 horsepower, thanks to a turbocharger producing up to 11.4 pounds of pressure. That was good enough, Porsche claimed, to rip the car from 0 to 60 mph in just 5.2 seconds. Over the years, the car would gain an intercooler, more gears (first five, then six speeds), all-wheel-drive, and another turbo. When *Motor Trend* drove an all-wheel-driven, $102,400 911 Turbo in November 1996, it burst to 60 mph in just 3.7 seconds.

"Imagine, 150 mph, with little fuss and the stereo playing. But what does all this mean in the U.S., with our present 55-mph speed limit? Why is Porsche even going through the paces? The immediate reason is economic, since Porsche feels it will have little trouble selling the 400 Turbos allocated for our market—with a price just under $26,000."

JANUARY 1975

Reflections on the Past: *Motor Trend* 25 Years Ago

Motor Trend celebrated its 25th birthday with an essay from the first editor, Walt Woron, among other recollections.

"It was a paradoxical period in which Motor Trend *was to be born. The war was over, but still it smoldered. Only now, it was a Cold War with Russia, threatening to erupt at any moment. There was a feeling of false security—engendered by our hellfire-and-brimstone 33rd President, Harry S. Truman..'Give 'em hell, Harry!' "*

MAY 1975 ▲

Preview: Rolls-Royce Carmargue

As Cadillac introduced its relatively expensive Seville, Rolls-Royce was showing its absolutely expensive Carmargue coupe. At $70,000, the Pininfarina-designed Carmargue was essentially a rebodied Silver Shadow sedan, and only 534 were built through '86.

"So let's wade in by saying that there are cars which will accelerate faster; there are some which will handle better; there are even one or two which, in specific circumstances, are even quieter. But in this writer's opinion, there are none which can rival the Carmargue's ability to transport its occupants in such splendid isolation."

◀ JUNE 1975

Pacer

The idea of the AMC Pacer was to add space to a short car by making it wider. The result of that idea was, well, ugly. It was also, at 3,375 pounds, heavy and, with only 110 horsepower from its 258-cubic inch inline six, underpowered. Despite that, AMC sold almost 200,000 of the bulbous cars during its first two years in production ('75 and '76). Then the market for the car tanked, and in its last two years ('79 and '80), despite an optional V-8 and a second wagon model, AMC couldn't quite sell 1,200.

"Our eyes are accustomed to a certain dimensional balance. The Pacer defies this balance. It really does look weird—from the outside. From the inside, it doesn't look weird at all."

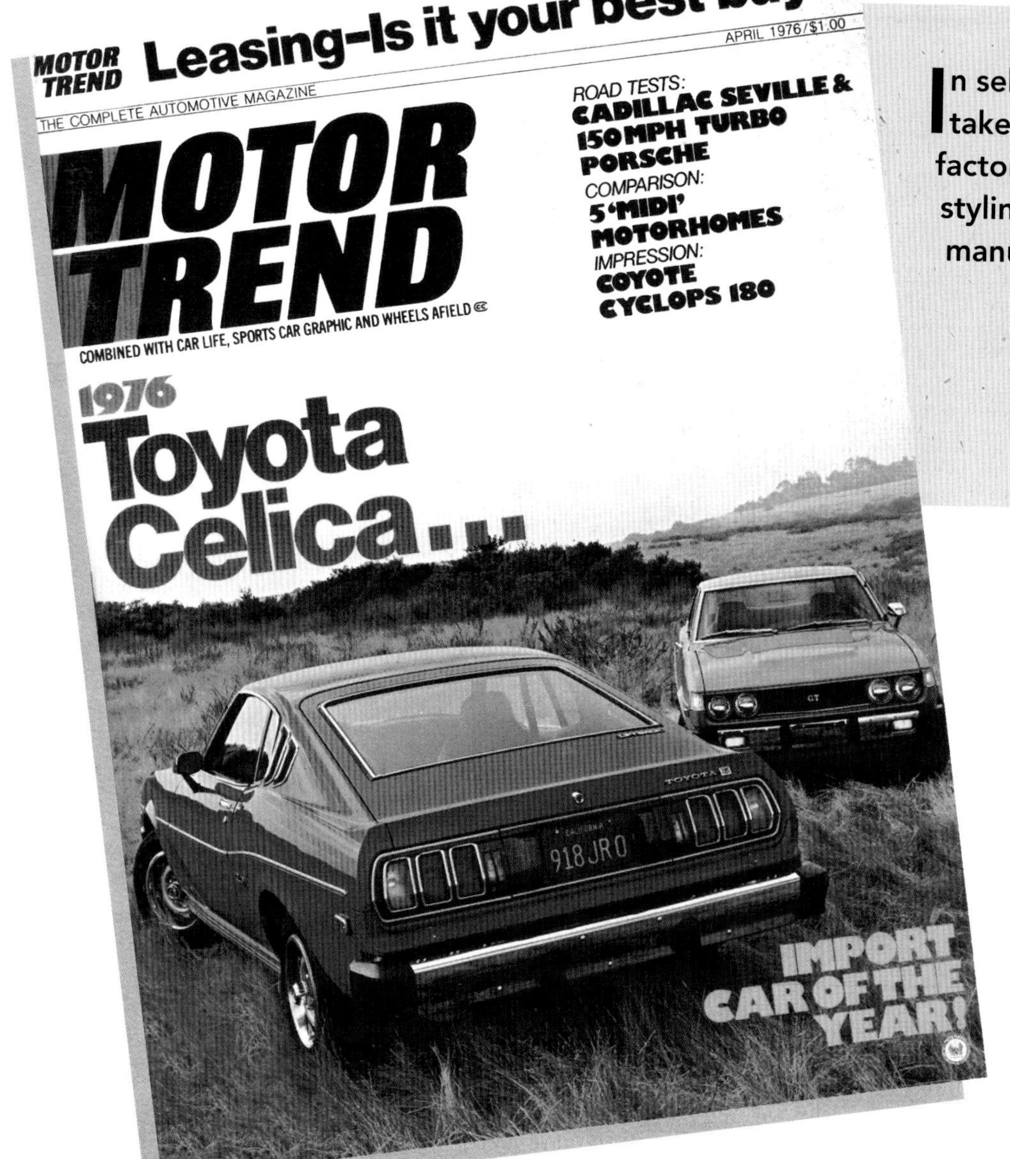
MOTOR TREND

Leasing–Is it your best buy?

UK 50p 02011

APRIL 1976/$1.00

THE COMPLETE AUTOMOTIVE MAGAZINE

MOTOR TREND

COMBINED WITH CAR LIFE, SPORTS CAR GRAPHIC AND WHEELS AFIELD

ROAD TESTS:

CADILLAC SEVILLE &

150MPH TURBO

PORSCHE

COMPARISON:

5 'MIDI' MOTORHOMES

IMPRESSION:

COYOTE CYCLOPS 180

1976 Toyota Celica...

IMPORT CAR OF THE YEAR!

In selecting the Import Car of the Year, we take into consideration many important factors. We look at the engineering, the styling, the overall concept, and how well the manufacturer executed it.

—"1976 Toyota Celica, Import Car of the Year" April 1976

JULY 1976 ▶

Comparison: The Van Affair

No fad during the '70s was quite as vivid or ubiquitous as the one that promoted full-size, modified vans as a lifestyle. Even *Motor Trend* couldn't avoid it in this comparison of big boxes from Chevrolet, Dodge, Ford, and GMC.

"A van will fit almost any lifestyle from camping to surfing, from cruising to commuting, and while there may be more than a little fadism involved in the current success of vans, it's safe to assume that vans and all the variations on the basic theme we have around us today are a permanent part of the automotive scene."

1976

◀ APRIL 1976

The All-New 1962 Avanti

Studebaker was gone, but Nate Altman wouldn't let the Avanti die. The South Bend, Indiana, entrepreneur took the car's tooling and kept building the stylish fiberglass coupe in small batches over GM drivetrains as the Avanti II.

"My feeling was that the Altman Avanti isn't exactly a sports car, but it's certainly on a par with a lot of so-called grand touring machinery around. Compared to some of the hotter ponycars of six or seven years ago, the Avanti II's performance and handling would be rather ordinary, but by today's standards, it's definitely a peppy item."

JUNE 1976 ▲

Buick's Turbo V-6

Facing the challenge of pacing the '76 Indy 500, Buick could have chosen to modify one of its oversize 455 V-8s back to muscle-spec and wedge it into the midsize Regal pace car (as it did for its '75 Regal pace car), but instead added a turbocharger to its familiar 3.8-liter V-6 to produced a 306-horsepower whoosher. No mere one-off, a more civilized version of the turbocharged V-6 would enter production for '78 and, with the addition of electronic fuel injection in the '80s, be used to power Buick performance legends like the Regal Grand National and awesome GNX.

"That diminutive V-6 would pull up to 120 mph and effortlessly hang there, not even breathing hard. I also made several full-throttle runs from 90 to 110 mph, which remember, is the crucial test. No problem for the turbo V-6. It repeatedly made the 90-110-mph move in 8 to 8.5 seconds. The '75 pace car took almost twice as long."

1977

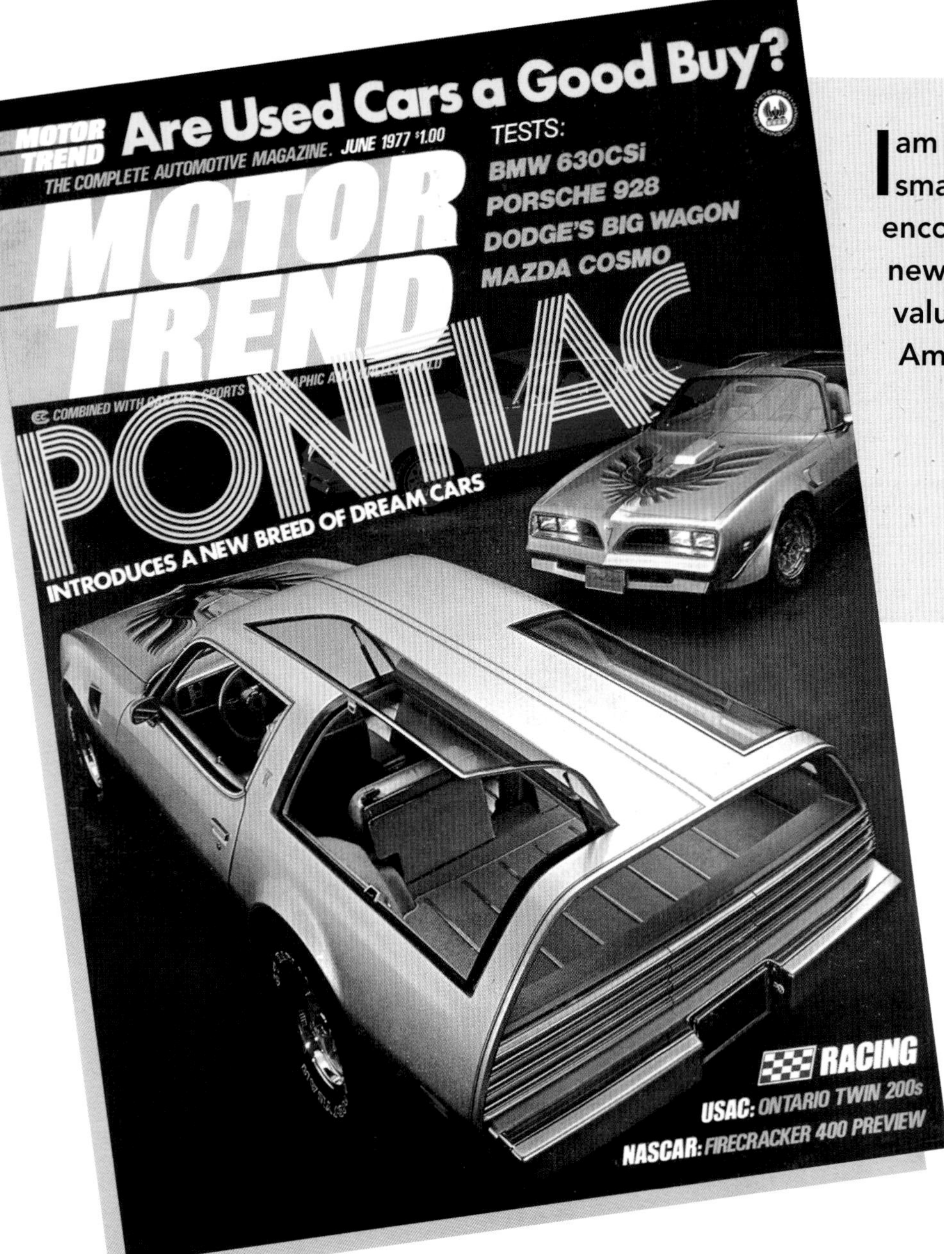

MOTOR TREND Are Used Cars a Good Buy?

THE COMPLETE AUTOMOTIVE MAGAZINE. JUNE 1977 $1.00

MOTOR TREND

TESTS:
BMW 630CSi
PORSCHE 928
DODGE'S BIG WAGON
MAZDA COSMO

PONTIAC INTRODUCES A NEW BREED OF DREAM CARS

RACING
USAC: ONTARIO TWIN 200s
NASCAR: FIRECRACKER 400 PREVIEW

I am confident by 1986 the average car will be smaller, lighter, and more efficient. DOT will encourage the public to voluntarily accept the new-style car. If our nation is to conserve valuable fuel and protect the environment, Americans will have no other alternative.

—William T. Coleman
U.S. Secretary of Transportation
"Cars of the '80s"
January 1977

APRIL 1977 ▲

Road Test: Ferrari 308 GTB

Ferrari finally brought a true successor to the beloved Dino 246 GT to the market in the mid-engine, V-8-powered 308 GTB. Unlike the disappointingly angular, four-seat, Bertone-penned Dino 308 GT/4, the Pininfarina-designed GTB was instantly recognizable as a Ferrari, a two-seater and sensuous in innumerable ways. The first GTB tested here, powered by a 3.0-liter/240-horsepower DOHC V-8, was also the first Ferrari with a fiberglass body. However, production quickly reverted to steel body construction, and the car would become available as a removable roof GTS and then eventually sprout fuel injection and four-valve heads. An increase in engine size to 3.2 liters inspired a name change to 328 in '85. The basic body shell was also used as the basis for the fabulous turbocharged '86 288 GTO.

"The real thrill of the 308 does not lie in how quickly you can launch it but in how quickly it can be motored once launched. This car, like the Dino, will quickly let you know that, unless you are very good, indeed, it exceeds your capabilities."

DECEMBER 1977 ▶

Silver Anniversary Corvette

With the introduction of the '78 Corvette (which featured most a new bubble-back rear window), America's one true sports car celebrated its 25th anniversary. *"While a quarter-century of longevity is remarkable for any vehicle out of Detroit, the Corvette represents a major miracle of survival over obstacles which defeated countless other makes and models. After all, the limitation of 'Polo-White and Powerglide only' wasn't much of an endorsement—even back in 1953.' "*

1977

SEPTEMBER 1977 ▲

Introducing the 1979 DeLorean—the Car and the Company

John Z. DeLorean's dreams of building his own car company rested squarely on the shoulders of this stainless-steel–skinned prototype in '77. Eventually an evolution of this prototype would enter production at a purpose-built Northern Ireland facility, not in 1979, but 1980. But the DeLorean project would prove star-crossed; the company collapsed amid a financial crisis in 1982, and DeLorean himself would endure a drug-trafficking trial (in which he was found not guilty), while the car went on to star in the "*Back to the Future*" movies.

"DeLorean will seek to build in values that other cars don't provide in so great a measure. Ritual annual model changes aren't likely at DeLorean, for example, at least not just for the sake of change. The car has been designed for model continuity. And the materials and construction methods have been selected to give long life."

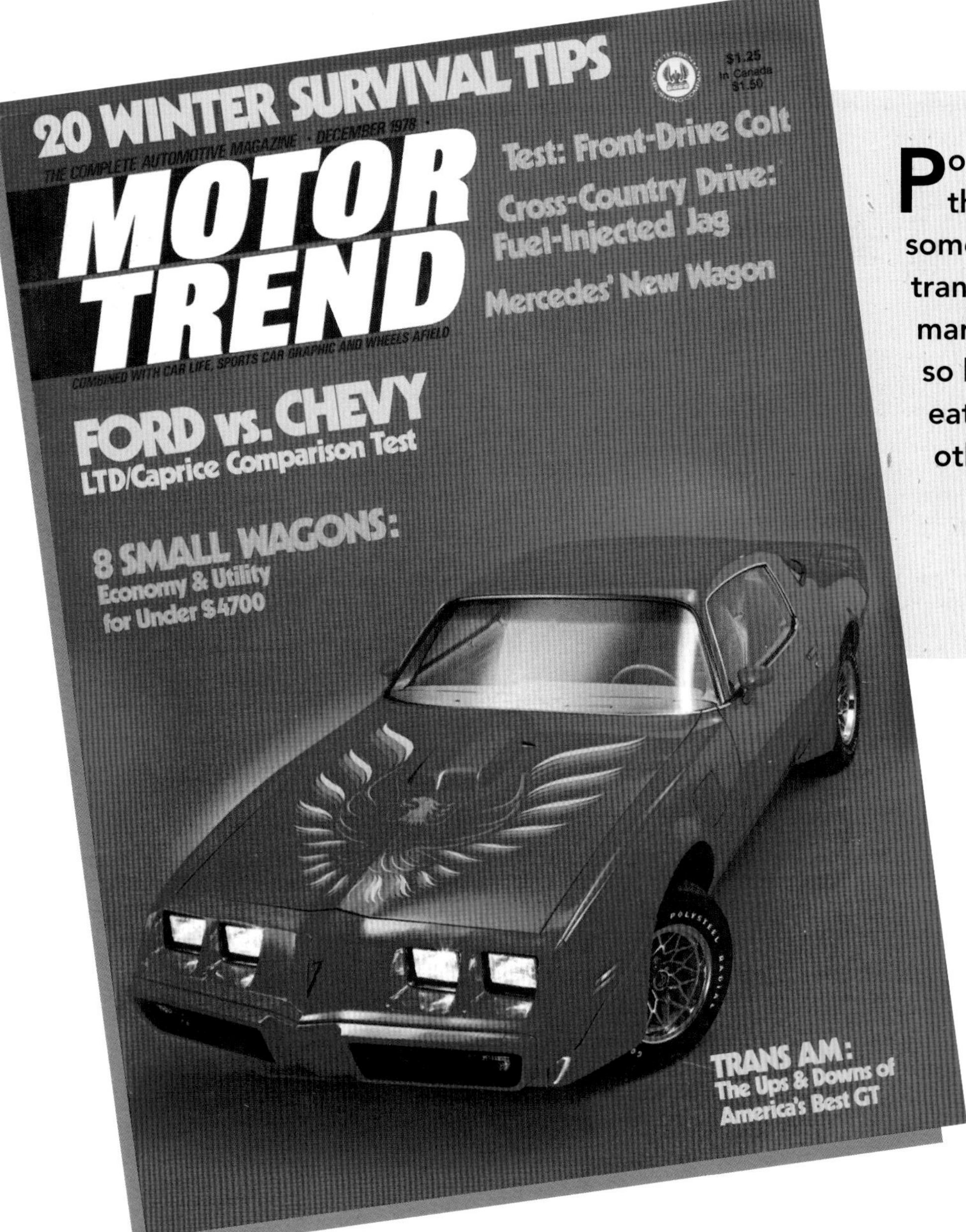

Pontiac determined through market research that the average T/A owner was born sometime in the late 1940s or early 1950s. This translated into what they termed the "youth market," a very special group filled with blood so loyal that a Trans Am owner would rather eat steel wool than drive a Formula, or any other Firebird model.

—*"Trans Am, the Last of the Supercars"*
December 1978

MAY 1978 ▲

Driving Impression: Mazda RX-7

Mazda finally found an appropriate home for its silken rotary engine in the first RX-7 sports car. The original RX-7 was a simple car (MacPherson strut front and a solid axle rear suspension), whose small size and instant reflexes were perfectly attuned to the rotary's swift responsiveness. On sale in June 1978 as a '79 model, the RX-7 prices started at just over $7,000.

"Acceleration with two aboard is quite good, considering the rated engine size of what the Japanese refer to as 35cid plus 2, the latter meaning 2 rotors. With the manual transmission and a standard 3.91:1 rear axle ratio, 0-60 time was 9.2 seconds, 16.7 for the quarter mile."

MAY 1978 ▲

Road Test: Porsche 928

Despite being among the very finest driving cars ever built, Porsche lovers would never accept the front-engine water-cooled V-8-powered 928 as a replacement for the beloved 911 or even as a "true" Porsche. The first 928 in 1978 used its 4.5-liter/219-horsepower SOHC to jog to 60 in 8.2 seconds and run the quarter-mile in 17.2 seconds at 87 mph.

"Front-mounted, liquid-cooled engine and silence of operation or no, the 928 is all Porsche, traditionalists notwithstanding. It is, after all, completely in the Porsche tradition of providing the ultimate in ground transportation for those who are unconcerned with carrying three children, a large dog, and a steamer trunk. The 928 is, in short, the best Porsche yet."

1978

◄ AUGUST 1978

Lotus Cars Ltd.

In 1978, Lotus Cars was at its peak. Besides having a line of wedge-shaped street cars consisting of the Esprit (in yellow), Eclat (blue), and Elite (white), the firm's founder, Colin Chapman, was revolutionizing the racing world with his ground-breaking, ground-effects Formula One cars. In fact in 1978, Mario Andretti would drive the Lotus 79 F1 car to that year's World Championship.
"Lotus has come a long way since Anthony Colin Bruce Chapman started building race cars in 1947. The transition has been made from track to street, from kit-form to full-production and, the latest, from boy racer to prestige car. It has all been part of Chapman's carefully thought-out master plan, with Esprit, Eclat, and Elite being the latest phase of this ongoing evolution."

◄ JUNE 1978

A Trio of Super Coupes

The definition of a performance car in the '70s had been expanded to include everything from tiny Civics through oversize sedans like Mercedes' S-Class. And the mainstream for performance cars was vehicles such as the "factory special" Honda Accord LX, Volkswagen Scirocco Sidewinder II, and Ford Fairmont ESO. But expectations for speed were diminished at the time. The 200-cubic inch six in the Fairmont made only 85 horsepower and that car needed a full 16.6 seconds just to make 60 mph. That was slow enough to make the 68-horsepower Accord's 15.2-second and 71-horsepower Scirocco's 14.6-second clockings for the same feat seem absolutely scalding.
"The Super Coupes are in. Affordable, reliable, and carrying the full manufacturer's warranty, factory modifieds are aimed at owners who want something different in a production car without the extra cost of having it done by an outside shop or the problems of getting it repaired either in or out of warranty."

NOVEMBER 1978 ▲

Datsun 280ZX

With the introduction of the '79 280ZX, what has once been Datsun's lithe sports machine transformed itself into a personal luxury machine with sporting overtones. But in the late- '70s context of diminished expectations, it was a huge hit.

"The 280ZX is totally new and probably the most innovative thing to come from Nissan steel. And more than that, it retains the basis for acceptance in the American market because the changes it has undergone deem the ZX a complete Grand Touring car, a road car in the best sense of the meaning. Nissan is so adamant that anyone overheard using the term 'sports car' will suffer bamboo under the fingernails."

1979

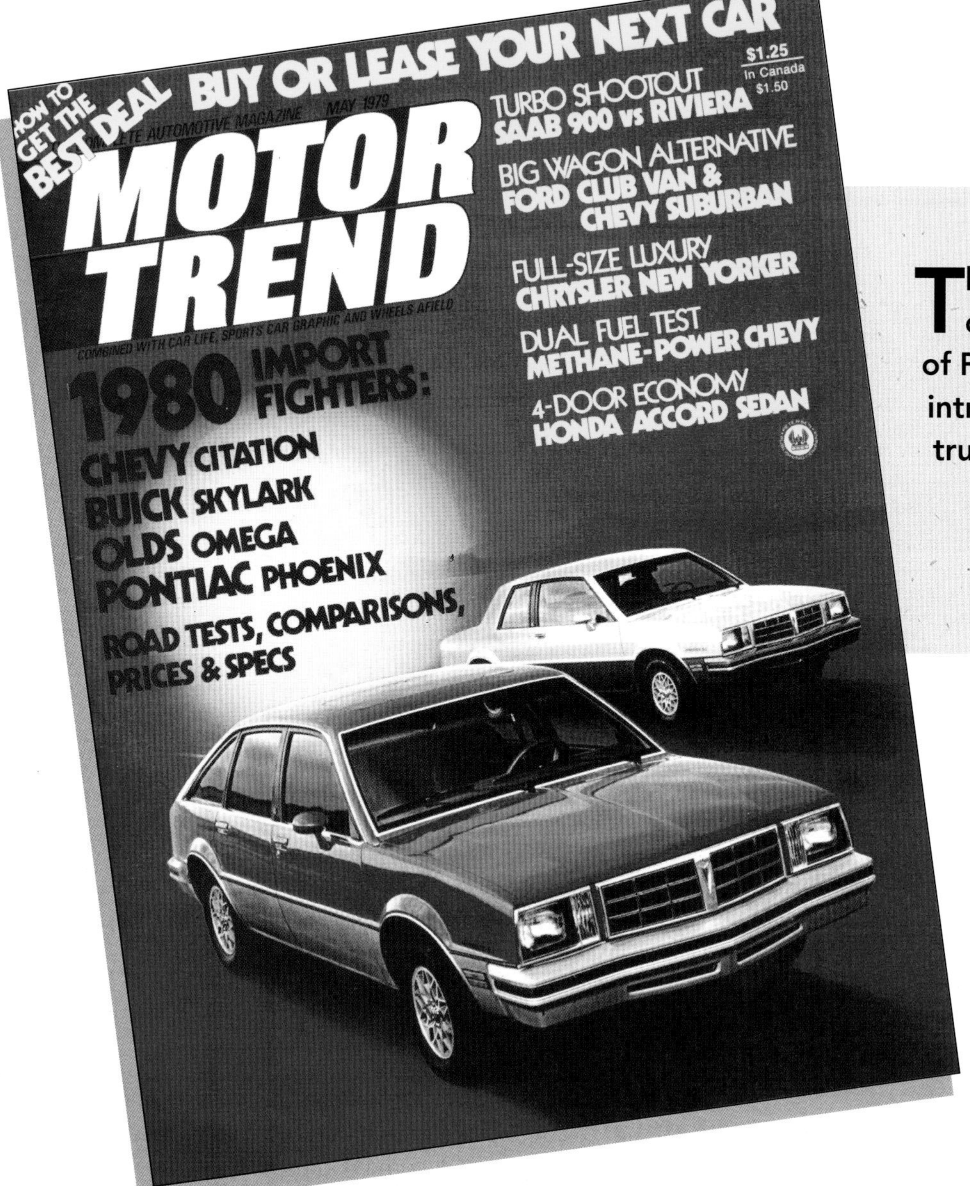

The importance of these automobiles cannot be overstated, for the entire future of Pontiac rests with them. They are introduced as 1980 models, and they are truly vehicles for the next decade.

—"GM's X Cars: Pontiac Phoenix"
May 1979

APRIL 1979 ▲

Mustang Turbo versus BMW 320i

Based on the Fairmont's "Fox" platform, the all-new '79 Mustang was more international in flavor and good enough to inspire *MT* to pit it against the leader in sport sedan fashion, BMW's 320i. While a 302 V-8 was available in the '79 Mustang, the most intriguing option was a 130-horsepower turbocharged version of the base 2.3-liter OHC four. With a four-speed manual trans aboard, that engine pushed the pony-car to 60 in a quick-for-the-day 10.6 seconds. But otherwise, the Turbo Mustang never lived up to its promise.

"What might have been hoped from the turbo is the free-revving red-line-in-every-gear performance associated with European turbo cars, notably the Saab. Unfortunately, the promise is never quite lived up to. Engine vibration is considerable, and the power seems better suited to highway passing situations than to performance driving."

NOVEMBER 1979 ▲

The Turbine Corvette

What did the Granatelli family do with the leftover turbine engines from their late-'60s Indy efforts? At least one of the 880-horsepower Pratt & Whitney ST6B turbines wound up in a Corvette, a Corvette that ripped to 60 mph in just 3.6 seconds! And destroyed the quarter-mile in 12.0 seconds at 111 mph.

"Massive ventilated NASCAR-style disc brakes were fitted to all four corners, a move made necessary by the fact that the car will, on level ground, idle at 60 mph. In around-town driving, the speed was controlled by applying the brakes rather than the throttle."

1979

JUNE 1979 ▲

Cat Tales in the Sunset

The XJ-S coupe had the unenviable task of replacing the beloved E-Type roadster and coupe in the hearts of enthusiasts when it was introduced for '76. It never did quite do that, but with Jaguar's 244-horsepower V-12 under its long hood, and a 0-60 time of 8.4 seconds, there was much to love about the $26,000 '79 edition.

"In spite of its flaws, the Jaguar XJ-S remains one of the finest mass-produced cars in the world. It has personality, presence, and a trait that's becoming rare in automobiles; character."

SEPTEMBER 1979 ▲

Road Test: TR7 Convertible

Triumph introduced its TR7 first as a '76 coupe, but it didn't become a credible member of the British sports car club until they whacked off the roof for '79 to create a convertible. However it was too late; even after installing the Range Rover's 3.5-liter V-8 in '80 to create the TR8, buyers had already moved beyond the wedge-shaped car. It would take the Japanese Mazda Miata a decade later to reinvigorate the passion that once was exclusive to British sports cars.

"In order to accommodate the TR7's slippery wedge shape, its 1998cc powerplant resides under the hood at a 45-degree angle. The 85.5-horsepower SOHC engine is a more conventional variant of the four-valve-per-cylinder stormer found in Triumph's Dolomite Sprint and emits that familiar, terribly British whine as it goes off in search of the 6500-rpm redline. It's capable of finding it, but in point of fact, the gutty little four-banger seems to lose interest in the hunt when faced with the prospect of turning anything over 5500 rpm. Our best quarter-mile pass netted 71.7 mph and 18.8 seconds, but the car creates a feeling of being moderately quicker."

20-Page Reader Swap Meet
SPECIAL SECTION
MOTOR TREND
AUDI 5000S TURBO
HONDAS: CAR vs. BIKE
BUICK SKYLARKS:
Sport Coupe & Sport Sedan
200-MPH
$200,000
American
Dream
Machine
MOPEDS: PEDALIN' FOR DOLLARS

4

THE 1980s

1980–1989

By the time Jimmy Carter signed the Loan Guarantee Act, which ensured Chrysler's survival in 1980, a revolution was already under way in Detroit. The business-as-usual assumptions that had proved so nearly disastrous during the '70s were being overturned. Everything that could be questioned was being questioned. GM and Toyota building cars together? Unimaginable during the '70s, and a reality in the '80s.

JULY 1985

Road Test: Ferrari Testarossa

Ferrari upped the supercar ante with its spectacular mid-engine Testarossa powered by a 5.0-liter DOHC 48-valve flat-12 knocking out 380 horsepower. Hit the throttle in this car, and you could feel the whole thing torque over. Fast? Zero to 60 mph took 5.3 seconds and the quarter mile thundered by in 13.4 seconds at 110.7 mph.

"Take the newest gem in the Ferrari crown: the 177-mph Testarossa with its 48-valve mid-mounted flat-12 and Can-Am-racer styling. Can there be any rationale for spending $87,000 on transportation? Yes, but only one: You have fallen absolutely and irretrievably in lust."

GM's go-it-alone tradition was abandoned when it signed a joint venture agreement with Toyota in 1983 to convert a recently closed GM plant in Fremont, California, to the production of small cars and trucks to be sold through both Toyota and GM dealers. Since 1985, the resulting New United Motor Manufacturing, Inc. (NUMMI) has been turning out Toyotas, Geos, and Chevrolets. Meanwhile, Chrysler and Mitsubishi opened an Illinois assembly plant under the name Diamond Star Motors in 1985, and Mazda and Ford began production at their Flat Rock, Michigan, AutoAlliance plant in 1987. International cooperation, once anathema to the Big Three way of doing business, was now eagerly pursued.

But cooperation didn't end competition. While the Big Three were establishing joint ventures, many of their manufacturing partners were opening plants of their own in the United States. While the Pennsylvania assembly facility Volkswagen opened in 1978 would ultimately prove a boondoggle and close, the Marysville, Ohio, plant opened by Honda in 1982 is still efficiently churning out Accords, while Camrys have been constructed in Kentucky since 1988. Subaru, Suzuki, and Isuzu would also begin or open North American plants during the '80s.

While all those new plants were going up, new technology was pouring into them. Computer-controlled robots automated more and more production processes during the '80s, resulting in both more consistent quality and a vastly improved plant flexibility. And much the same computer technology that was revolutionizing manufacturing was changing the vehicles themselves.

GM's '80 X-Cars—the Chevrolet Citation, Buick Skylark, Pontiac Phoenix, and Oldsmobile Omega—represented that corporation's first indication of what an '80s car would be. They were smaller than their predecessors, powered by four- and six-cylinder engines rather than sixes and eights, and front rather than rear drive. And over the rest of the decade, GM would convert the vast majority of its car lines over to V-6 power and front drive. What had been the defining features of an American car, a big V-8 in front driving the rear wheels, were vanishing.

Over at Chrysler, the money it secured with the government's guarantee went into producing the front-drive K-Car line. Introduced in '81 as the Plymouth Reliant and the Dodge Aries, the K-Car couldn't have been more prosaic, a square box with simple mechanical bits. But up against the wall as it was, Chrysler would twizzle that box into everything from convertibles and luxury cars to, most impressively, in '83, the minivan. So successful were the K-Car's derivatives that the company was able to repay its loan guarantees after only three years—seven years ahead of schedule. The K-Car may never go down as a classic, but it saved Chrysler.

Ford started the '80s stocked with cars that were almost parodies of boxiness. But boxiness wasn't selling, and in '83, with a new Thunderbird, it began to define a fresh, aerodynamic look that reached full expression in the ground-breaking front-drive '86 Taurus. The Taurus wasn't just all-new, it looked all-new, and, even better than that, to customers it immediately appeared all-better. In the marketplace, the Taurus' presence was electrifying; it shifted the expectations of customers about what a domestic, mainstream sedan could and should be. It reminded the entire world how capable the Big Three could be if they tried. And it renewed Ford's confidence.

As much as things changed on the outside of cars, the biggest changes were under the hood. When the '80s began, carburetors were used on most cars. By the end of the decade, virtually every car used computer-controlled electronic fuel injection, and many were also featuring computerized transmissions and/or anti-lock brakes and traction control.

The precision afforded by electronic engine controls meant that, even though emissions standards grew more stringent throughout the decade, unlike in the '70s, engines wouldn't necessarily lose power. In fact, it was often the case that engines would run cleaner while gaining power and becoming more fuel efficient as such electronic powertrain-management systems were adopted. For example, the carbureted 350-cubic inch (5.7-

liter) V-8 in the '80 Chevrolet Camaro Z28 was rated at 190 horsepower, while the same size V-8 in the '89 Z28 with GM's "Tuned Port Injection" electronic fuel-injection system produced 235 horsepower. And the '89 engine produced more low-end torque, had much better drivability, and was generally more reliable.

Although cars changed dramatically during the '80s, and in most ways for the better, buyers increasingly turned to trucks. Besides Chrysler's ground-breaking minivan, sport utility vehicles such as the small Chevrolet Blazer and Ford Bronco II were attracting buyers who wanted a good chunk of rugged image enhancement alongside the practical advantages of a truck. But the biggest winner in the '80s SUV race wasn't Ford, GM, or Chrysler.

Amid a dispiriting partnership with France's Renault, AMC's Jeep division developed a new compact-size Cherokee for '84. Unlike the other domestic SUVs against which it competed, the Cherokee used unibody construction and was available with four doors. Those four doors made the Cherokee not just another SUV, but a direct alternative to the traditional station wagon as a family vehicle and the prototype for all SUVs of the '90s. Since its introduction, the Cherokee and its derivatives have reinvigorated Jeep as a prestige brand in American motoring. The rest of AMC was a basket case, but the Jeep brand was suddenly so attractive that Chrysler acquired the company in 1987.

Wave after wave of change washed through the motoring world during the '80s, and *Motor Trend* reported each one. Yet it was all only a tantalizing hint of what was to come.

FEBRUARY 1980

Motor Trend's 1980 Car of the Year

The Chevrolet Citation and its fellow GM X-Car stablemates, the Pontiac Phoenix, Buick Skylark, and Oldsmobile Omega, are not coveted by collectors today, but they set the pattern for most domestic sedans to follow in the '80s. That includes front-drive, four-cylinder, and V-6 drivetrains, and greater commonality of parts.

"The Citation became Car of the Year in much the same way that Jody Scheckter became World Driving Champion: It scored well with consistency. With the Citation, GM and Chevrolet have redefined automotive basics in a fresh, totally American way."

1981

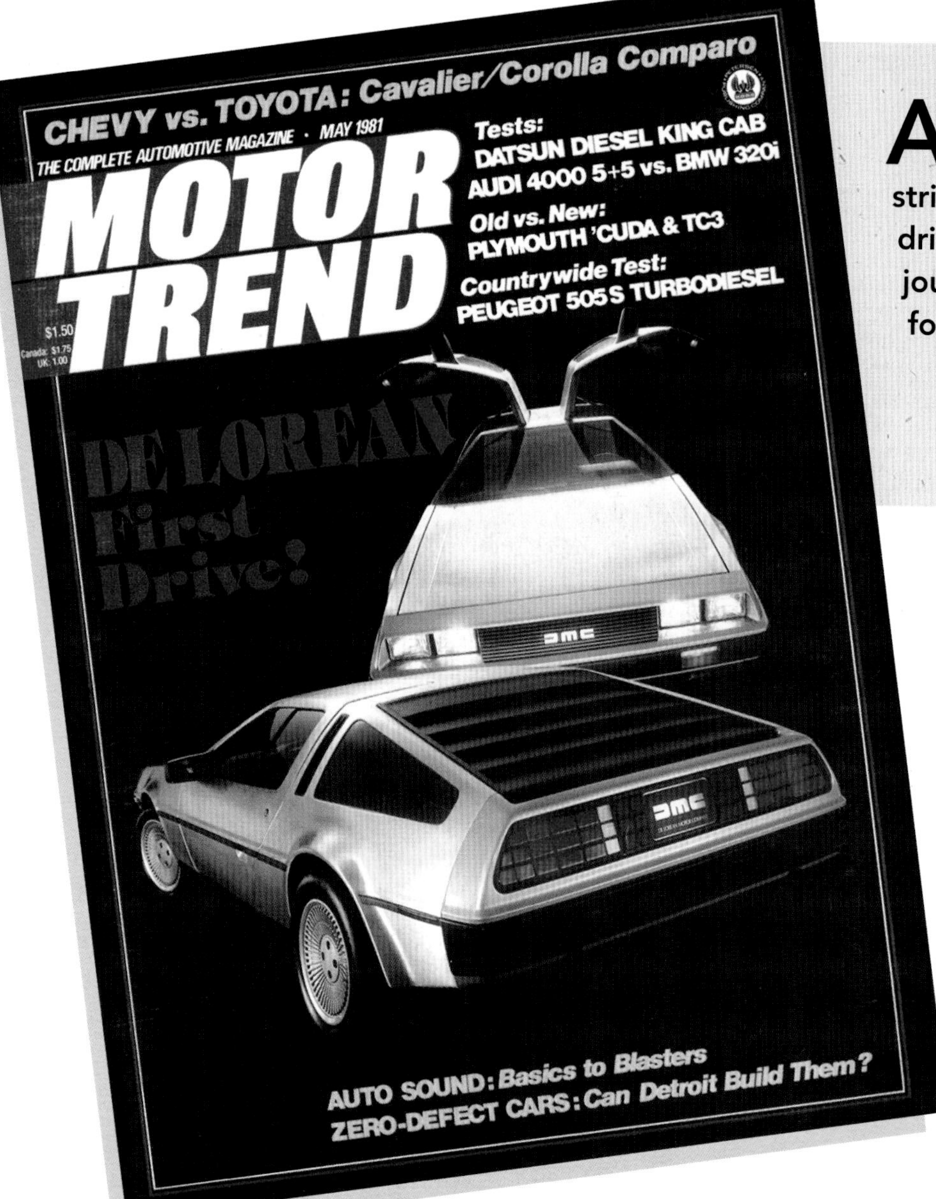

All things considered, the De Lorean has a lot in its favor. The appearance is striking. It's very sporty and rewarding to drive, yet comfortable and relaxing on long journeys. And on top of this it should last forever and a fortnight.

—*"De Lorean"*
May 1981

FEBRUARY 1981 ▶

1981 Car of the Year Winner: Chrysler K-Car

This ordinary-looking car saved the Chrysler Corporation, and it gets no respect for doing so. Over the '80s, as much out of desperation as true inspiration, the basic front-drive K-Car (Dodge Aries and Plymouth Reliant) would be modified into dozens of different and distinct vehicles, most notably the market-shattering minivan. Today, any K-Car gets little notice; back then *Motor Trend* knew how important it was to Chrysler and how good it was in the context of the time.

"The thing we liked best about the K-Car was the amount of overkill built into the vehicle that must satisfy such a large segment of the market. The standard suspension has more bravura than any normal driver will ever use, though at speeds under 40, it is mellow and compliant. On the open road, the K acclimates itself accordingly, exhibiting a taut-feeling ride, minimal body roll, maximum steering input, and a great feel for the road."

JUNE 1984

Doin' It in the Dirt

Rally driving legend Rod Millen needed an all-wheel-drive car to compete against the Audi Quattro John Buffum was then using to dominate the SCCA Pro Rally series. What he built was this four-wheel-drive Mazda RX-7.

"At the end of the day, it was finally our turn to drive the RX-7 on these wonderful dirt roads. We were not disappointed. After some detailed instructions like: 'Just stand on the gas,' and 'it goes where you point it,' we eased the clutch out and lurched off, spraying everyone with dirt and rocks. The straight-cut transmission gears whine like a siren, and the dust tastes terrible. Oops, pay attention, here comes the first corner. Wow, this is fun! Sliding around at impossible angles, we began to appreciate some of the things Rod had told us about driving with all four wheels."

1982

Ford has an excellent opportunity to expand its chunk of the growing specialty car segment with the new Thunderbird. The new car's combination of shape, style, handling, and luxury is more than enough to erase the humdrum record of the Bird it replaces.

—*"First 1983 Test, 1983 Ford Thunderbird"*
October 1982

FEBRUARY 1982 ▲

Royal Roll-Off: Cadillac Seville vs. Lincoln Continental

In engineering, the front-drive Seville and rear-drive Continental shared little. But they were both aimed at the same market, and they shared a certain awkward bustle-back styling that left the market cold. Both would eventually be replaced by cleaner, smaller designs. *"While Cadillac appears more interested in holding onto its traditional market, Lincoln-Mercury looks upon the '82 Continental as a conquest vehicle. By slanting it toward a bit younger, more adventurous buyer, L/M hopes to snare a few borderline free spirits who can often be seen lurking about Cadillac dealerships."*

JUNE 1982 ▲

Road Test: Audi Quattro

Audi took the dive into all-wheel drive with its limited-production '82 Quattro, a car aimed as much at rally drivers as the buying public. Power for the coupe came from a 160-horsepower, turbocharged, SOHC five, while the all-wheel-drive system itself used a concentric driveshaft and center differential. All-wheel drive, in the form of the "Quattro" option, continues to be a hallmark of the Audi experience.

"The Quattro elevates the German firm's basic success formula to previously unattained heights. Looking rather like a Coupe that's been put through an intensive body-building regimen, the Quattro was designed to serve as Audi's technological showcase for the '80s. It succeeds brilliantly in that role. More important, it ranks as one of the finest all-weather GT machines on the market today."

1982

MAY 1982 ▲

Road Test: Camaro vs. Mustang

The all-new, third-generation Camaro was big enough news in '82 that the Z28 earned MT's Car of the Year award. But Ford fought back with a new, more powerful 5.0-liter V-8 for its Mustang GT, and the result was an escalating performance war throughout the rest of the decade. The initial face-off between the 145-horsepower 305-cubic inch V-8 four-speed '82 Z28 (0-60 in 8.6 seconds, the quarter-mile in 16.7 at 81.0 mph) and the 157-horsepower 302-cubic inch V-8 four-speed '82 Mustang GT (0-60 in 7.8 seconds, the quarter-mile in 16.3 at 83.7 mph) only hinted at the performance yet to come. For enthusiasts, things were starting to change for the better.

1982

"Performance—the grand old American variety—has pulled its foot back out of the grave and now looks to have a surprisingly bright future. Even if that future won't produce 426 Hemis again, under the heat of competition and age-old adversarial relationships, it will certainly stimulate some widespread attitude adjustment among today's driving enthusiasts."

1983

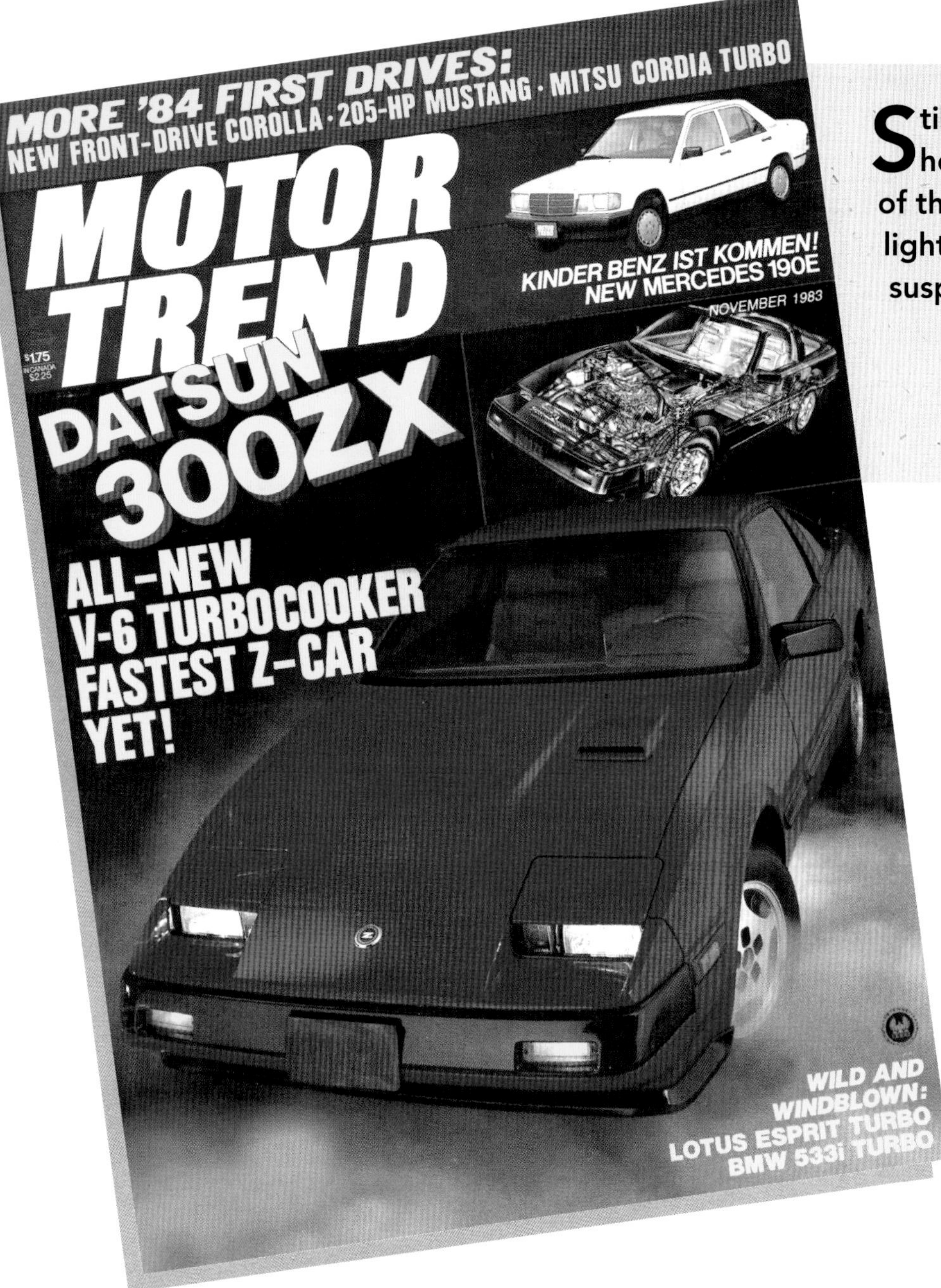

Still there is this unfulfilled desire, around here anyway, to see a Z-car more in the vein of the original 240, a stripped-down, lightweight streetfighter, a take-no prisoners suspension, a car abuzz with tactile input.

—"1984 Nissan 300ZX Turbo"
November 1983

APRIL 1983 ▸

Mid-American GT Revival

By 1983, one would have thought the "Win on Sunday, sell on Monday" logic that led to factory racing efforts was dead. But NASCAR was growing in popularity, Detroit found that Americans still loved racing, and cars like the slope-nosed Monte Carlo SS made sales sense. The nose on the SS would make the car an instant success in NASCAR Winston Cup competition, but the street car's L69 190-horsepower four-barrel-topped 305-cubic inch V-8 meant performance was rather modest—but quicker than that of the Camaro Z28.

"Though we tried a number of driving and launching techniques and a variety of shift points, the first run of the day with a cool engine and a warm track surface proved best: 0-60 in 7.97 sec, 0-70 in 10.15 sec, a quarter mile in 16 sec flat at 85 mph, and a top speed just over 120 mph (at 5600 rpm in high gear)."

◀ JULY 1983

The *MT* Ragtop Revue

In 1981, it seemed convertibles were doomed. By '83, *MT* was able to gather a full dozen of them, including new drop-top versions of the Ford Mustang, Porsche 911SC, Pontiac 2000 Sunbird, and Buick Riviera. What they did with them was as much a staff communal adventure up California's coast as an actual test. *"Obviously, we were having far too much fun. It was time for something more like work, specifically a few rides through a local car wash, in Santa Barbara. The* Motor Trend *Monsoon Test is simple: Cars go into the wash, and the driver rides along watching for leaks. In some cases, this didn't require much watching—the observation could be carried out even with one's eyes closed. Of the 12 convertibles, only the Buick, Rolls-Royce, and Volkswagen made it through with no leaks. Both the Aston and the Mercedes-Benz allowed a minute bit of seepage from the top of the door glass on one side. The Chrysler, Fiat, and Porsche leaked from the tops of the side windows on both sides. The Alfa Romeo, Excalibur, Mustang, and Pontiac Sunbird exhibited leaks from the tops of door windows, rear quarter windows, and even the windshield header."*

1984

The 1984 Porsche Carrera Turbo-Look is a lot of things. It's too expensive, too red, and too fast. It's also ego-inflating, sensuous, rewarding—and beautiful.

—*"Porsche 911 Carrera Turbo-Look"*
May 1984

DECEMBER 1984 ▶

Road Test: Pantera!

Despite rumors to the contrary, the Pantera was not dead and reappeared in the United States as the Pantera GT-5. Still powered by Ford's 351-cubic inch V-8, but now sourced out of warehouse stocks in Australia, the "Sport" version rated at 350 horsepower. Why is the lady in the black dress walking a panther on the beach? Why not?

"The Pantera performs like a '85 Corvette: 0-60 mph in under 6 sec, 0-100 in about 15, the quarter mile in the mid-14s at almost 100 mph. Top speed on TRC's 7.5-mile banked bowl was an rpm-limited radar-confirmed 138 mph. With the alternative 4.01:1 differential ratio instead of the 4.22:1 of our test car, the Pantera would pick up some top speed, to perhaps 150, at the expense of acceleration."

1984

1984

FEBRUARY 1984 ▲

Car of the Year, 1984

In a year featuring the debuts of the ground-breaking Chrysler minivans and Pontiac's rule-breaking, mid-engine Fiero, it was still little surprise that the fourth-generation Corvette walked away with *MT's* highest honor for '84.

"Somewhen, somewhere, when we're all zooming around in anti-grav land speeders and lateral g is a forgotten concept, it's going to be interesting to go to the archives and see what's been written about the '84 Corvette."

OCTOBER 1983 ▲

1984 Dodge Caravan

Once-precarious Chrysler redefined what a family vehicle could be with its most creative variation on the K-Car, the '84 minivans.

"Dodge's new Caravan and its Plymouth Voyager runningmate will open the new selling season in a class by themselves. Neither Ford nor Chevy is expected to have a competitive product ready until the '85 model year, though several Japanese challengers, led by Toyota, will be stepping forth considerably sooner. After a five-year gestation period, Chrysler's big gamble appears ready to pay off. If so, the firm should find itself on the inside track to a market segment that analysts feel will be one of the hottest of the '80s."

JANUARY 1984

Family Fourwheelers

Minivans weren't the only emerging family transportation in '84; SUVs were making a play for the kids-and-stuff market. *MT* gathered some mainstream players in the form of Chevy's Blazer S-10, the Ford Bronco II, Jeep Cherokee Chief, and Mitsubishi Montero Sport. Though all were two-doors in the test, at that time only the Cherokee was available as a four-door.

"The Jeep Cherokee—the newest arrival in this class, and a vehicle that simply did too many things too well to be ranked as merely a match for the others. It outperformed all comers in instrumented testing; it gave the nicest ride on all surfaces; it kept the best in sight through the nastiest, steepest, axle-bustingest terrain we threw at it; it offered the greatest cargo capacity (by both volume and weight); and when the occupant count rose above two, it was clearly the most accommodating."

SEPTEMBER 1984 ▲

Road Test: 1984 Pontiac Fiero

The mid-engine two-seat plastic-bodied Fiero was a tantalizing small car and the only product Pontiac could claim as having to itself alone. But it was also a car that would prove fatally flawed in its archaic, 92-horsepower "Iron Duke" four-cylinder engine, unfortunate Chevette-derived front suspension, and substantial quality problems. All those deficits would be addressed during the car's five-year production run, but not before it had already failed in the marketplace.

"With the sole exception of the '84 Corvette, no car in recent memory has generated as much preintroduction speculation as this one has. The spy photo/rumor merchants have been going full-tilt since word first got out that such a car was scheduled for production. We've been waiting for this one a long time, and for lots of good reasons."

JULY 1984 ▲

The *MT* Flat-Out Follies

Given enough road, how fast would the 240-horsepower tuned port-injected '85 Corvette, 235-horsepower Ferrari 308GTBi Quattrovalvole, 205-horsepower Lotus Esprit Turbo, 200-horsepower Porsche 911 Carrera, and 234-horsepower Porsche 928S go? Surprisingly, the car that had been the quickest in '83, the 928S, was the slowest in '84, making it "only" to 147.1 mph on the 7.5-mile track at Ohio's Transportation Research Center, while the Carrera hit 149.7, the Ferrari 151.3, the Lotus 152.0, and the Corvette an awesome 155.2 mph.

"Many claims are bandied about concerning top speed, and it's not too surprising, because it's one thing to speculate about absolute top end, quite another to prove it. Manufacturers' claims of 150 mph can't be investigated by running out to our normal testing facility and standing on the gas. At 150 mph, a vehicle gobbles up a football field every 1.33 sec; or, put another way, it covers our normal test facility's entire straightaway in under 10 sec."

1984

◀ AUGUST 1984

SVO Mustang

Ford's Special Vehicle Operations (SVO) was responsible for the design and production of a special '84 Mustang. Running an advanced, fuel-injected version of Ford's turbocharged 2.3-liter four-cylinder engine producing an impressive 176 horsepower, this car was designed to compete with European makes in levels of refinement and sophistication. But the parallel to Carroll Shelby's development of the GT350 Mustang of two decades earlier was too obvious to ignore. *"The '84 Mustang SVO's athletic abilities are truly to be commended, and by any realistic standard, it is inarguably the 'better' all-around automobile of these two. Certainly, as a product to sell to the public in the year 1984, the SVO would be the one to bet on. For that matter, a sporting machine with the SVO's talents and its civility would have been a huge hit in 1965, too."*

1985

FINALS '85 IMPORT CAR OF THE YEAR

MOTOR TREND

GUANCI: THE MID-ENGINE CORVETTE

MARCH 1985

1986 FORD TAURUS

FoMoCo Reveals the Shape of Tomorrow

TESTS: NEW BMW 535i, HONDA CRX Si

No doubt about it, Ford has a winner on its hands. With a projected base price of less than $10,000 and an estimated out-the-door median of $13,000, the Taurus is taking dead aim at the GM A-car and Chrysler E-series.

—"Preview, 1986 Ford Taurus"
March 1985

With cheese-slicer side gratings, a wedge-shaped profile, and blocky (for a Ferrari) lines, the Testarossa inspired as many detractors as admirers. Featuring an estimated top speed of 175 mph and 13.3-second quarter-mile times, the Testarossa was introduced at the Paris Auto Show in 1984 and went into production in 1985.

1985

◄ SEPTEMBER 1985

Porsche 959

A full 14 years after its debut, the Porsche 959 remains, arguably, the most technologically advanced production automobile ever built. Only 200 copies of the 959 were built at a price of $130,000 each and none was certified to operate on American roads. Having seen how the 959 was built, even at that price, it's assumed Porsche took a loss on every car. *"Do we exaggerate when we call the 959 the fastest, most advanced ever? Not likely. A combination of specs-reading and seat-of-the-pants reckoning leaves little doubt: a 450-hp twin-turbo race-based engine drives 2900 lb. through a 6-speed gearbox and all four wheels; electronics constantly regulate the fore/aft torque delivery, as well as differential locking, shock damping, and ride height; Kevlar bodywork has been slicked down to a 0.32 Cd, which the 956-derived powerplant can push to some 190 mph. Not bad for something the engineers will tell you is not particularly intended for racing applications."*

APRIL 1985 ▲

Track Test: Gloy Sports Capri

The SCCA's Trans-Am road racing series experienced a renaissance in the mid-'80s, but with tube-frame full race cars instead of the modified ponycars that ran in its muscle-era heyday. The 1984 series champ Tom Gloy's Mercury Capri was based on the Bob Riley-designed chassis that dominated the series throughout the decade under Capri, Merkur, and Mustang bodywork, whether with V-8 or turbo four-cylinder power. With a 305-cubic inch racing V-8 aboard making about 550 horsepower, the Gloy car ripped to 60 in 3.98 seconds. Writer Ron Grable was able to hot lap the car around California's Sears Point Raceway road course.

"With our test day's track conditions, Tom managed a 1:42, and we had worked our way down into the 1:45s when we did a no-no. Coming past the pits after exiting the turn 11 hairpin, we executed a beautiful shift 4th to 5th—but got 3rd instead. The rev limiter protected the engine, but, of course, it had to happen directly in front of the pits, and the collective scowls deepened a couple clicks. So, reluctantly, we decided our time in this championship Trans-Am car should be over."

1986

MOTOR TREND

10 TESTS: Alfa, BMW, Buick GN, Eldorado, Isuzu, Merkur, Mustang, Seville, Suzuki, T-Bird

MOTOR TREND

THE WORLD'S AUTOMOTIVE AUTHORITY

ALL-NEW ASTON MARTIN ZAGATO

JUNE 1986

EXCLUSIVE! Jet vs. Vette

Chuck Yeager Testpilots 200-mph Corvette

FIRST LOOK! CADILLAC'S ELEGANT ALLANTE

The twin-turbo Corvette is an experimental prototype that will never see the light of a production line and, as such, will remain beyond the reach of most of us. Not so the T-38. Thornton Enterprises makes this particular brand of fantasy available to everyone. That's right, you can ride in this thing.

—*"The Adventures of Super Jet and Turbo Vette"*
June 1986

AUGUST 1986 ▶

Hollywood Vice

The ultimate '80s TV show? *Miami Vice.* The car driven on that show? At least during the first season, it was a black Ferrari Daytona Spyder replica built atop a Corvette chassis. *Motor Trend* drove a clone of that car, built by McBurnie Coachcraft of Santee, California, and writer Jack Nerad indulged his fantasies. *"So to deal in the high-dollar world of contemporary crime, when I took the assignment of journalist-in-residence for the Hollywood police force, I needed a car that expressed my individuality, my taste, my savoir-faire. Call me Johnny Crickett: I'm a detective for Hollywood Vice."*

1986

1987

These vehicles represent the absolute highest speed potential available to the European buyer. We decided to answer the question of which is the fastest of the fast, and gathered together the Ferrari Testarossa, Lamborghini Countach, Porsche's new 928S 4, and the Lotus Esprit Turbo, for a trip to Transportation Research Center.

—"Europe's Fastest of the Fast"
January 1987

1987

OCTOBER 1987 ▶

Chevy's Super-Secret SuperVette

By '87, rumors of a wildly more powerful, mid-engine Corvette were swirling around Detroit, and that led to some thrilling speculation. At the time, Chevy was deep into Indy car racing, and a mid-engine exotic seemed a natural extension and celebration of that success. But there's still never been a mid-engine Corvette, even though the DOHC 32-valve LT-5 V-8 discussed in the article did make it into the '90-'95 ZR-1 "King of the Hill" Corvette.

"Cooperative GM sources close to the exotic Corvette program provide the minute details that confirm the accuracy of these Duane Kuchar illustrations. Engineers are the first to remind us that any automobile pegged for the '90s might be described in 1987 as 'Silly Putty.' Funding flux, engineering direction changes, even personnel shifts all affect the final version of a highly complex sports car scheduled three to five years away."

◀ DECEMBER 1987

Road Test: Oscar Mayer Wienermobile

Test drive the Oscar Mayer Wienermobile? Why not?

"There's the immeasurable quantity known as status that surrounds you like a halo when you're at the wheel of the Wienermobile. Suddenly the world becomes your condiment table. Pretty girls flock to you; successful men salute; and children stick to you like pickle relish. Ferraris, Lamborghinis, and even Chrysler New Yorkers fade into nothingness when the Wienermobile arrives. You need never worry about getting parking spot No. 1 at a fancy restaurant because you're driving a fancy restaurant."

1987

SEPTEMBER 1987 ▲

Road Test: BMW M6

BMW's 6-Series coupe was already more than a decade old when the lusty $59,000 M6 appeared in federalized form with BMW's famed 3.5-liter DOHC 24-valve S38 Motorsport inline-six providing power. Developed for racing, S38 powered a series of successful BMW sedan racers and then found a home in the M1 sports car of the early '80s. In the United States-bound M6, the S38 was rated at 256 horsepower, which was down about 10 percent from its European output. But it scooted the M6 to 60 mph in 6.9 seconds and revolutionized *MT's* performance expectations for luxury coupes.

"The harder you press the throttle pedal, the harder it gets to criticize the cost of the M6. And you can press it all the way to 145 mph. But it's not the big numbers that impress most; it's the forceful rapidity with which the M6 stretches out and grabs them."

1987

APRIL 1987 ▲

Driving Impression: Regal GNX

Buick had built turbocharged 3.8-liter V-6s since '78, but nothing quite like the limited-production Regal GNX. Fiddling with the turbo plumbing and engine control computer resulted in a turbo engine rated at 300 horsepower and 0-60 times in the mid-5-second range. It took nearly $30,000 to buy a new GNX, which was undoubtedly the quickest Buick ever. And it will take at least that much to buy one today from a collector.

"This car accelerates hard enough to get into triple-digit speeds right now. In such situations the driver needs to devote all his attention to the job at hand, and shouldn't be required to hang onto the steering wheel to stay upright—that's the function of the seat. Please, Mr. Buickman, a killer seat for a killer car."

1988

Say you're too scared of the thing to ever drive it. No problem. What sounds like more fun: investing in some boring piece of property someplace, or having an F40 on full-time static display in your garden house? If you ever got your courage up, driving the car would just be gravy.

—*"Inside the Ferrari F40"*
July 1988

DECEMBER 1987 ▸

Road Test: BMW M3

BMW's $34,000 M3 debuted in the United States as an '88 model powered by a high-tension 2.3-liter/192-horsepower DOHC 16-valve four. It was a race-bred car produced to homologate it for the European touring car competition. And its thoroughbred instincts were uncompromised and instantaneous. The six-cylinder M3 that replaced it in the '90s would be more civilized, less ferociously focused, and even more fun to drive.
"After hot-lapping the racetrack and getting comfortable at speed, the drive back to the city was akin to someone letting the air out of your balloons."

1988

DECEMBER 1988 ▲

Rambo's Lambo

No production off-roader was, is, or may ever be as radical as Lamborghini's ultra-aggressive, $125,000 LM002. With the Countach sports car's 4.8-liter/332-horsepower DOHC 48-valve V-12 in its nose, and humongous 325/65VR17 tires at every corner, the Lambo was amazingly capable off-road and a stunning presence on-road. *"It's actually pretty nimble, in a three-ton milk truck kind of way. It weighs 6173 lbs., so a lightweight it ain't. On dirt surfaces, you can even hang the tail out if necessary, but more often than not you must induce this just for the fun of it. The Lambo's 315 lb-ft of torque maxes quickly at 4500 rpm, so you can climb over anything the brush-bustin' tubular front bumper will clear."*

◀ MAY 1988

Road Test: Porsche 944 Turbo S

Though unloved by Porsche traditionalists, few cars in the '80s drove better than the front-engine, water-cooled 944 Turbo S. The big 2.5-liter SOHC four pressurized by a single turbo produced a shockingly easy-to-use 247 horsepower. It was mated to a chassis that had been thoroughly developed into one of the best-balanced cars in the world. The trip 0-60 mph took a scant 6.6 seconds.

"The S-model option adds $5298 to the 944 Turbo's bottom line, putting the grand total perilously close to $50,000 out the door. For most of us, the idea of spending 50 grand on a sports car doesn't come under the heading 'cautious personal financial planning'—it's just a touch extravagant. But look at it another way: Imagine you were considering the regular 944 Turbo, but discovered you could have the faster, tighter-handling S model for just 10 percent more. Judged in that light, the 944 Turbo S can only be considered a bargain. Regardless of the price, the Turbo S happens to be the best-balanced sports car Porsche builds."

APRIL 1988 ▶

1988 Import Car of the Year

Motor Trend's '88 Import Car of the Year is already now considered a classic of small-car engineering: the Honda CRX Si. This tiny, two-seat front-driver was an intoxicating mix of sporting flair and absolute practicality. Handling was nearly viceless, build quality extraordinary, and there was nothing else like it on the market.

"The new line of all-aluminum 4-cylinder Civic engines displays impressive performance in all trim levels. But it's the top-line 1.6-liter variant under the CRX Si's low-slung hood that really shines. Fitted with Honda's PGM-FI multipoint injection, this free-revving 16-valve SOHC gem develops over 90 percent of its maximum 98 lb-ft of torque as low as 2500 rpm. Mated to a crisp-shifting 5-speed gear-box, it powers the high-spirited CRX Si from 0-60 mph in under 9 sec and still earns 29/36-mpg city/highway marks from the EPA."

SEPTEMBER 1988 ▲

Top-Speed 10

If you could get a Ferrari Testarossa (175 mph), Porsche 928S 4 (165 mph), Chevrolet Corvette (156 mph), Nissan 300ZX Turbo (153 mph), BMW M6 (149 mph), Chevrolet Camaro IROC-Z (148 mph), Toyota Supra Turbo (147 mph), Mercedes-Benz 560SEC (143 mph), Ford Mustang GT (142 mph), and Pontiac Firebird GTA (141 mph) in one place at one time, you'd want to see how fast they could go, too. Especially if that one place was the 5.7-mile oval at Nissan's Arizona Test Center.

"What does it all mean? One thing seems obvious: The vehicles are clearly capable of much higher safe speeds than our system allows. And one thing that's not so obvious—it's fun."

1989

This is a serious for-real sports car that churns up all sorts of wonderful memories of late, great roadsters. The only difference is that this one is a far better, more capable car. And it even starts in the morning. For a newer generation of drivers who don't have those bittersweet motoring experiences to look back on, the Miata is ready to make them from scratch. Just add sun.

—"Motor Trend Road Test, Mazda MX-5 Miata" July 1989

JUNE 1989

Road Test: Corvette ZR-1

The plan was for the Corvette ZR-1 to enter production in '89, but it was delayed—after the press introduction of the car—until '90. So this test is of a very rare bird indeed; the pre-production '89 ZR-1. Of course, the essence of the ZR-1 was the fabulous 5.7-liter/380-horsepower DOHC 32-valve LT5 V-8, a powerplant developed by Lotus, built by Mercury Marine, and at least as exotic as that in any European mid-engine machine. It was inserted into a Corvette with widened haunches to cover vast P315/35VR17 rear tires and carrying a price tag almost $20,000 greater than the "regular" Vette. Through its life, the LT5's output would grow to 405 horsepower as it left production in '95.

"With a top speed in the neighborhood of 175 mph, a 0-60 time of 4.71 sec and 13.13-sec/110.0-mph quarter mile, no one's going to accuse the DOHC Vette of being limp-wristed."

1989

MARCH 1989 ▲

Road Test: Pontiac 20th Anniversary Trans Am

With a 3.8-liter/250-horsepower turbocharged V-6 from the Buick Grand National, the very limited-production 20th Anniversary Trans Am is now considered as much a classic as any other Trans Am, including the original '69 with which it was photographed. Only 1,500 were built, and each was likely capable of duplicating the MT test car's 5.4-second 0-60-mile-per-hour rage and 14.2-second at 95.8-mile-per-hour quarter-mile performance.

"It's forceful, focused, and—we have to admit—imperfect, but it brings a real excitement to driving, an excitement that's all too often missing lately in the corporate-think insurance-wary world we live in. Make no mistake, this is a modern, sophisticated vehicle—usually that means boring—that'll smack ya back into the seat like a '60s musclecar and gets 20 mpg. Like having your cake and eating it, too."

1989

NOVEMBER 1989 ▲

Driving Impression: Shelby Dakota V-8

Restlessness defines Carroll Shelby's life. Extending a relationship with Chrysler, Shelby shoehorned a 5.2-liter/175-horsepower (318-cubic inch) engine into the Dodge Dakota midsize pickup to create a personal-use truck with sporting appeal. Shelby built fewer than 2,000 Dakotas, but primed the pump for a '90s boom in muscle trucks.

"When it comes to the drive, the Shelby Dakota keeps its truck identity. Though you won't feel like you're riding a bull elephant, you also won't feel like you're in an average car."

1989

FEBRUARY 1989

1989 Car of the Year

With an all-independent suspension beneath it and a 3.8-liter/210-horsepower supercharged V-6 propelling it, Ford's all-new '89 Thunderbird Super Coupe was a big, confident road machine. Just the sort of car with which to enter the '90s flying *Motor Trend's* Car of the Year banner. However, the '90s would not be kind to coupes in general, and throughout the decade the T-Bird would face dwindling sales. It left production after '97, but the name awaits revival as a retro-styled two-seater in 2001.

"The Thunderbird levels its competition. Nothing else in the price range offers the same irresistible blend of sporting performance and solid luxury."

DECEMBER 1989

Road Test: Mercedes-Benz 300SL & 500SL

Introduced to Europe in 1989, the impregnable six-cylinder 300SL and V-8 500SL roadsters made it to America for the '90 model year.

"For the first time, Mercedes is offering SL buyers a choice of two engines, each an electronically fuel-injected DOHC gem with 4 valves/cylinder and variable valve-timing to help extract maximum performance. The 300SL uses a 2962cc inline six based on the same 3-liter powerplant found in the 300E, but here fitted with an all-new aluminum head. It develops 228-hp. Those in search of the ultimate M-B performance car will have to opt for the awesome 500SL. Its 4973cc all-aluminum V-8, which spawned the current Group C race engine, makes 322 hp. Our formal acceleration testing merely confirmed what we already knew to be true: This baby is part rocket. Blasting 0-60 mph in 6.1 sec and flashing through the quarter mile in 14.4 sec/100.4 mph, it possesses bona fide supercar credentials in an unbelievably refined package."

BONUS: EXOTIC CAR CALENDAR!
DECEMBER 1990
FIRST DRIVE! 202-MPH DIABLO!
MOTOR TREND
TOP SPEED SHOWDOWN
ACURA NSX
DODGE STEALTH
MITSUBISHI 3000GT
NISSAN 300ZX
TOYOTA MR2
ROAD TESTS:
PORSCHE 928 GT
MERCURY TRACER LTS
NISSAN 240SX
CADILLAC BROUGHAM

5

The 1990s

1990–1999

Welcome to the automotive golden age. The '50s had more extravagantly styled cars, the '60s, their own powerful exuberance, but the cars, trucks, SUVs, and whatever elses of the '90s are—as a whole and by far—the best built, best designed,

SEPTEMBER 1990

Road Test: Acura NSX

Exotic cars had been notoriously finicky until the Acura NSX appeared late in '90 (as a '91). From its brilliantly rigid all-aluminum structure, through its phenomenally capable mid-engine chassis and on to a 3.0-liter DOHC 24-valve V-6 incorporating Honda's VTEC variable valve-timing system to produce 270 eager horsepower, the NSX set new standards for supercars in its combination of world-class performance and everyday utility. Every sports car since—particularly Ferrari's F355—has been better because of the example the NSX set.

"It's the best sports car the world has ever produced. Any time. Any place. Any price. It's more of an achievement now than the Mercedes 300SL Gullwing was in its time-frame, more of an advance now than the Porsche 928 was in the mid-'70s. It's far better than any Ferrari or Lamborghini ever built; it makes the Corvette ZR-1 look like something contrived under a shade tree."

JUNE 1990 ▲

Trends: Detroit Report

No car had more visual impact than the Dodge Viper prototype shown first at the 1989 Detroit Auto Show. The radical 8.0-liter V-10-powered roadster was audacious even only as a prototype (seen here). Whether Chrysler would have the chutzpah to put it into production had the speculation generator working overtime. *"We don't believe the maybe-yes/maybe-no stuff emanating from Chrysler about the Viper sports car project. A speculator might theorize that, since Dodge will begin selling the twin-turbo Stealth supercar this fall, Eagle, with no American-built cars to its name, can use some ego of its own."*

most engaging ever. Performance cars have never performed better, utility vehicles have never been more useful, and luxury cars never more luxurious than during the last 10 years of the century. If speed is your measure of progress, the quickest production car of '88, the Ferrari Testarossa, went 175 mph, while '99's quickest car, the Ferrari 550 Maranello, did 194.

The auto industry's technological investment during the '80s paid off in the '90s. Flexible production techniques have allowed manufacturers to derive everything from coupes to sedans, minivans, and SUVs from common component bundles. Toyota's '99 Solara coupe, Avalon large sedan, Sienna Minivan, Lexus ES 300 luxury sedan, and Lexus RX 300 SUV, for example, all trace their engineering heritage back to the mainstream Camry. But one is hard-pressed to find how any of those vehicles is seriously compromised by its genealogy. In fact, they're better for it in many significant ways.

Electronic engine controls have resulted in innovations like electronic-variable-valve timing, which can be tuned for either high performance or economy. Honda's pioneering VTEC variable-timing system, for example, is used on both the near-exotic '99 Acura NSX mid-engine sports car, where it helps a normally aspirated 3.2-liter V-6 produce fully 290 horsepower, and in the Honda Civic HX coupe to deliver an EPA-rated 35 mph in the city and 43 mph on the highway while producing a commendable 115 horsepower from just a 1.6-liter four.

Dozens of technologies that seemed exotic in the '80s—anti-lock brakes, electronic traction control, sequential fuel injection, multivalve engines, low-profile tires—are common in the '90s on not just up-market vehicles but economy cars and mini-pickups. In fact, since '93, every new gasoline-powered vehicle sold in the United States has been fuel injected, and since '95, anti-lock brakes have been standard on Chevy's least expensive car, the Cavalier.

What's most surprising about the cars and trucks of the '90s, though, is what hasn't changed: Virtually all of them are still powered by internal-combustion piston engines fueled with gasoline. No atomic cars, no turbines, no vegetable-burning rotaries; anyone from the '50s could be propelled forward 40 years in history and still recognize the basic components of a '90s automotive powerplant.

Internal combustion survives, despite a relentless search for an alternative. Thanks to "Zero Emission Vehicle" legislation in states such as California, Honda, Ford, Nissan, Toyota, Chrysler, and, most prominently, GM produced electric vehicles for sale and/or lease to the public. But despite incorporating every conceivable innovation, ultimately, battery technology still wasn't (and isn't) up to the job of automotive fuel storage. Outside of various government agencies, few buyers were found

JULY 1990

Traction Control

Electronic traction control became increasingly popular throughout the '90s. Most systems incorporate sensors that detect a speed differential between front and rear wheels (and/or side to side), and then moderate throttle and/or apply brake accordingly until traction is restored. Many traction-control systems are integrated with anti-lock brake (ABS) installations.

"It would seem clear that, just as ABS offers considerable margins of braking safety and is now accepted as a major safety advance, traction control can offer the same increase in controllability for non-braking operations. As such, it unquestionably increases overall safety for the vehicle occupants."

for electrics, and Honda, for one, abandoned its electric vehicle production in mid-1999. Internal combustion is still the best combination of cost, efficiency, and infrastructure around.

Besides the technological revolution, the automotive landscape has changed with new manufacturers and marketing divisions. In '90, Toyota launched its Lexus, and Nissan its Infiniti luxury divisions, while Korea's Kia and Daewoo have fought to establish their presence in North America. And General Motors' brand-new Saturn division sold its first small car on Oct. 25, 1990, from a new Saturn dealership using new sales techniques that got its car from a factory running with a cooperative United Auto Workers labor agreement.

During the '70s and '80s, it seemed obvious that the cars of the '90s would be small, light, and the result of engineering undertaken in an era of diminished expectations. No one predicted that American consumers would be enchanted by not just trucks, but big trucks.

America's best-selling vehicle has been Ford's F-Series pickup throughout the '90s; during '98, Ford sold 836,629 of them. And at the same time, Chevy, GMC, and Dodge were all selling record numbers of full-size trucks. But pickups were only part of the story.

◄ DECEMBER 1990

Fast Five

By late-1990, Japan was producing cars of undeniable performance. In addition to MT's '90 Car of the Year, the Nissan 300ZX Twin Turbo (top speed, 158.7 mph) and the amazing Acura NSX (167.6 mph), the Toyota MR2 Turbo (144.2 mph), the fundamentally identical twin-turbocharged all-wheel-drive '91 Dodge Stealth R/T Turbo (153.1 mph), and Mitsubishi 3000GT VR-4 (162.2 mph) were on sale. MT took all five out to answer the question, "Wot'll she do?"

"These five marvelous sports cars have been introduced within the past year or so, which means each was conceived under the potential specter of increasingly unfavorable actions from the regulationists. Each represents a considerable act of not only engineering achievement and conceptual innovation, but of faith and gumption, as well."

Throughout the '90s, America's families increasingly sought out SUVs and trucks as alternatives to traditional sedans and station wagons. Trucks such as the Ford Explorer, Jeep Grand Cherokee, Dodge Durango, and Chevy Blazer SUVs became the mainstream choice for family transportation. And even the Chevy Suburban, once thought so gargantuan that only commercial users would dare buy it, was adopted by more and more individuals for daily transportation. During the 1984 model year, Chevy sold just 37,928 Suburbans. In 1998, it sold 107,708.

In such a rapidly evolving world, *Motor Trend* has kept up. In 1996 it launched both *Motor Trend* Online (www.motortrend.com), which soon became one of the most popular sites on the Internet and a gateway for thousands of people seeking automotive information on the Worldwide Web, and "*Motor Trend* Television," a half-hour program now on the Speedvision cable network. In 1998, *MT* grew four ways when it added *Truck Trend* and *Truck Trend* Online (www.trucktrend.com), a bimonthly magazine and Web site for truck buyers and enthusiasts; established the *Motor Trend* Driver's Association, whose members get discounts on automotive products and services, including emergency roadside assistance; and opened the *Motor Trend* Auto Program, which brings low, "no hassle" new-car pricing to anyone with a telephone. Once solely a magazine, *Motor Trend* is now a full-fledged multimedia enterprise.

What place will personal transportation have in the future? A future where a trip to the mall can be replaced with Internet retailing; where work is done with e-mail rather than a daily commute; where yes, eventually, the oil might run out and global warming may become an ever-more serious concern. And what will twenty-first century consumers, raised on 100,000-mile tuneups and ever higher quality cars, demand from future vehicles? As it was in 1949, it will be *Motor Trend's* job and privilege to report on and relish the motorized future.

1991

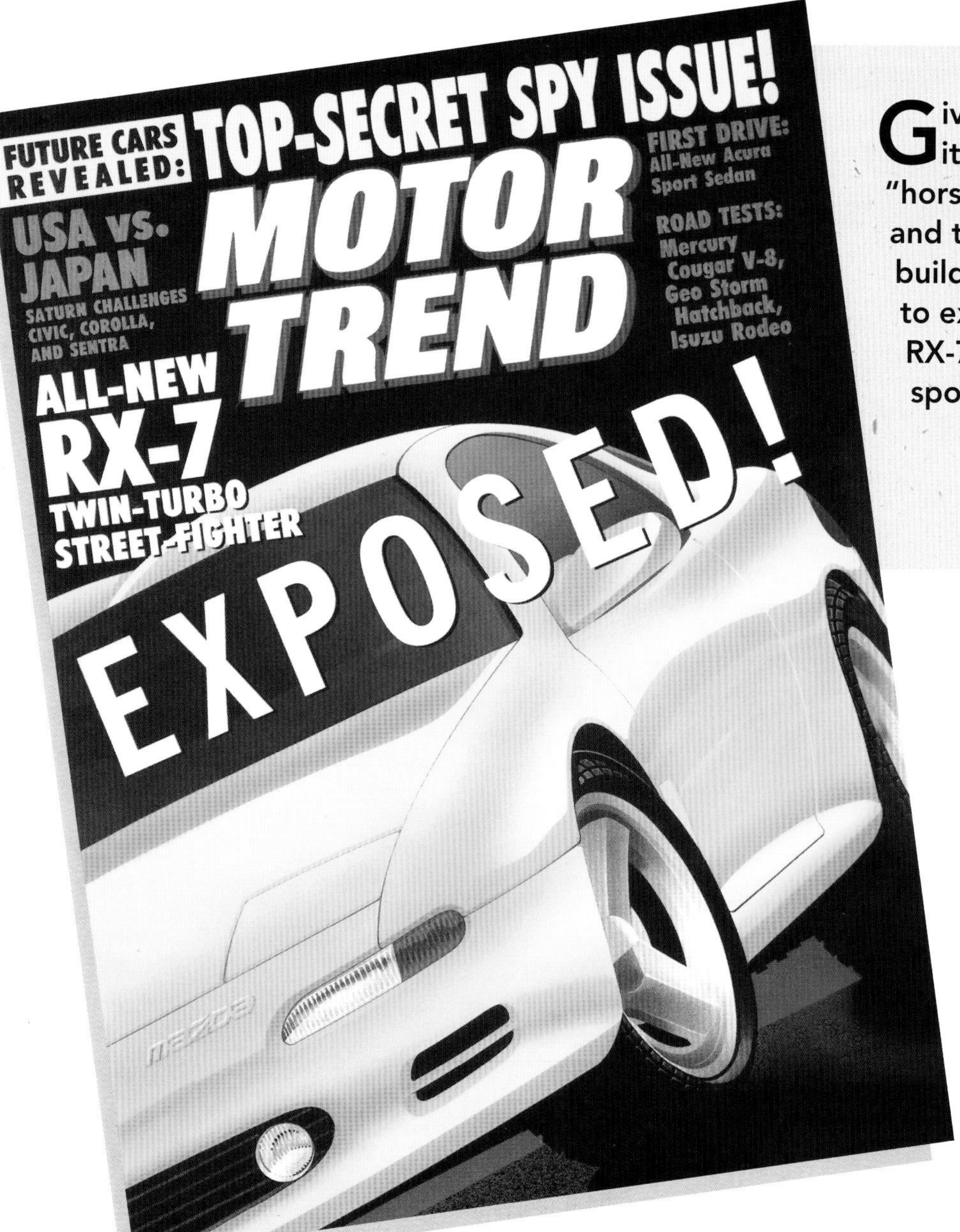

Given the success of the Mazda Miata, and its underlying concept of maintaining a "horse and rider" relationship between the car and the driver, we can expect the RX-7 to build upon this idea. It wouldn't be out of line to expect this new, lighter, more powerful RX-7 Turbo to be one of the best feeling sports cars in history.

—"Sneak Peek, Mazda RX-7 Turbo"
April 1991

1991

◀ MARCH 1991

1991 Truck of the Year

In the history of *Motor Trend's* "of the Year" awards, none has met with more controversy than the selection of the Mazda Navajo in 1991. Not so much because the Navajo was unworthy, but because the fabulous all-wheel-drive GMC Syclone, powered by a 4.3-liter/280-horsepower turbocharged V-6, didn't win. That's despite supercar performance like a 4.9-second rip to 60 mph and a 13.6-second/98.6-mile-per-hour quarter-mile blast. But a truck is not a supercar.

"For all its speed and road prowess, the Syclone does have its downside, reflected by low subjective scores. Judges complained about the GMC's uncomfortable fixed seatbacks, high level of interior noise, and substantial turbo lag. The most common criticism could be summed up on one judge's comment that the Syclone sacrifices 'truckness' to go overboard on 'carness,' gleefully abandoning the truck heritage. With a lightweight 500-pound load rating and no rated towing capability, 'nuff said."

SEPTEMBER 1991 ▶

4x4x4

For Ford, what the Mustang was to the '60s the Explorer SUV was to the '90s. Consistently the best-selling SUV in the world, the Explorer has become ubiquitous in mall parking lots and funneled untold billions into Ford's coffers.

"Ford's big, gentle bear is the newest, but follows in philosophical lockstep the older American's path. It's handsomely styled, substantial, and imparts a feeling of security, but is definitely skewed toward the street in terms of utility."

1991

MARCH 1991 ▲

BMW M5 vs. BMW 750iL

Few of us have ever been presented with the dilemma of choosing between the intoxicating high performance of the $56,600 310-horsepower DOHC 24-valve inline-six BMW M5 or the imposing luxury of the $74,000 296-horsepower SOHC 12-valve V-12 BMW 750iL as our sole means of sedan transportation. And what a dilemma to have.

"Comparing the two to each other, the M5 is faster and the 750iL smoother at roughly $20,000 more. We like the M5 because of its character and racing heritage. It's so fast it makes your eyes water, and that's enough for us."

1991

JULY 1991 ▲

Mitsubishi Diamante LS vs. Acura Legend Sedan LS

Somewhere between the expense and performance of high-end European luxury sedans and the overbearing plushness of traditional American luxury cars developed the mid-level luxury machines from Japan that tried to balance the two. Mitsubishi's $30,395 front-drive Diamante LS featured a DOHC 24-valve 3.0-liter V-6 making 202 horsepower, while the $34,596 Acura Legend LS relied on a 3.2-liter/200-horsepower SOHC 24-valve V-6.

"When you can buy the Mitsubishi's Diamante LS luxury automobile and stuff away a hearty certificate of deposit toward the kids' education for less than the sticker price of a Legend—experiencing a high degree of performance in the bargain—there's little left to discuss. Mitsubishi's Diamante is a car that shines among its peers."

1992

When the discussion's over and it's time to go drive, there's no waffling: The Viper is our candidate for 1992 king of the hill. Long live the King.

—"Viper Versus Vette"
February 1992

AUGUST 1992 ▶

Cobra 427 Reborn

After watching innumerable kit-carmakers copy his original creation, Carroll Shelby "uncovered" some unused chassis components and started up his Cobra 427 production line once again. With at least 425 horsepower aboard and the ability to corner at 1.02 g, the "continuation" Cobra, built to S/C "Semi-Competition" specs and priced at a blinding $500,000, performed significantly better than had the Cobra 427 (non-S/C) tested by MT back in '66. Zero to 60? That took 5.3 seconds in '66 and only 4.8 in '92. In '66, the quarter-mile flew by in 13.8 seconds at 106 mph, and in '92 it took only 13.2 at 105.6 mph. The parallel in quarter-mile trap speeds indicates that much of the difference in performance is likely due to tire differences; the better '92 rubber was able to hook up where the '66 doughnuts just spun. *"No doubt there will be lengthy arguments about whether Carroll's 'new' Cobra is a 'real' Cobra. That's not for us to decide. We're just thankful that ol' Shel' is still around to stir the pot one more time."*

1992

AUGUST 1992

Honda Prelude Si vs. Mazda MX-6 LS

The art of Japanese coupe-making reached a peak during the early-'90s with cars ranging from the Nissan Sentra SE-R right up to the sleek Lexus SC 400. But as the decade wore on, coupes fell further and further out of the limelight in favor of sport sedans and SUVs. In '92, however, Honda's 2.3-liter/160-horsepower DOHC 16-valve four-fired Prelude and Mazda's Michigan-built 2.5-liter/164-horsepower DOHC 24-valve V-6-powered MX-6 were right in the Japanese front-drive coupe mainstream.

"If a choice must be made, the MX-6 not only holds the edge in every measured performance category, but our testers felt it provides the best balance between performance, styling, and liveability. True to the current trend, the new Mazda has leap-frogged to the top of the class."

1993

"Okay," you ask, "so which is the winner?" If top speed is the sole judging criterion, the ZR-1 wins. If acceleration is the only yardstick, the Viper takes top honors. If you're a stoplight-to-stoplight street racer who never runs beyond 40 mph, the Typhoon gets the gold, ditto if you like to drag race in the rain. Biggest bang for the buck goes to the Z28, with the Firebird right behind.

—*"American Performance Car Shootout"*
June 1993

JUNE 1993

Chevrolet 454 SS vs. Ford Lightning

Unlike the severely focused compact GMC Syclone, Ford's SVT Lightning and Chevy's 454 SS were full-size trucks that worked quite well as trucks and performance vehicles. Chevy used its 454-cubic inch big block V-8 to put 255 horsepower into the half-ton, $22,219 454 SS, while Ford used a tuned sporting development of its 351-cubic inch V-8 to equip the $22,202 Lightning with 240 horses. But the Lightning was also a more fully realized vehicle, with a well-developed suspension on 17-inch wheels, cost slightly less, and, though it posted an identical 7.2-second 0-60 time as the Chevy, was slightly quicker in the quarter-mile (15.6 at 87.4 mph to 15.8 at 84.7 mph).

"A tally of the MT judges' ballots quickly gave us a winner: the Lightning. While the Chevy's tire-burning torque is big fun, there's a penalty to be paid at the gas pump. The muscular Ford, on the other hand, delivers slightly better performance, vastly superior handling, far greater towing capacity, and the best bucket seats ever put into a production pickup."

1993

FEBRUARY 1993

Shootout: Mustang Cobra vs. Camaro Z28

The fabulous fourth-generation GM F-Car (Chevy Camaro and Pontiac Firebird) appeared in '93, packing, in their high-performance guises, a full 275 horsepower from their 5.7-liter LT1 V-8 engines, six-speed manual transmission, four-wheel anti-lock disc brakes, and the best handling yet seen on a ponycar. To go up against the new Z28, Ford offered the specially tuned SVT Mustang Cobra with an improved version of the legendary 5.0-liter V-8 rated at 235 horsepower and a modified suspension wearing 17-inch wheels and tires. The $19,812 Camaro was quicker to 60 (5.6 to 6.2 seconds) and in the quarter-mile (14.0 at 98.8 mph to 14.4 at 97.4 mph) than the approximately $19,990 Cobra, and dominated the braking, skidpad, and slalom courses as well.

"No envelope needed—we have our winner. The Camaro Z28 is lord and master of the '93 ponycar arena."

1994

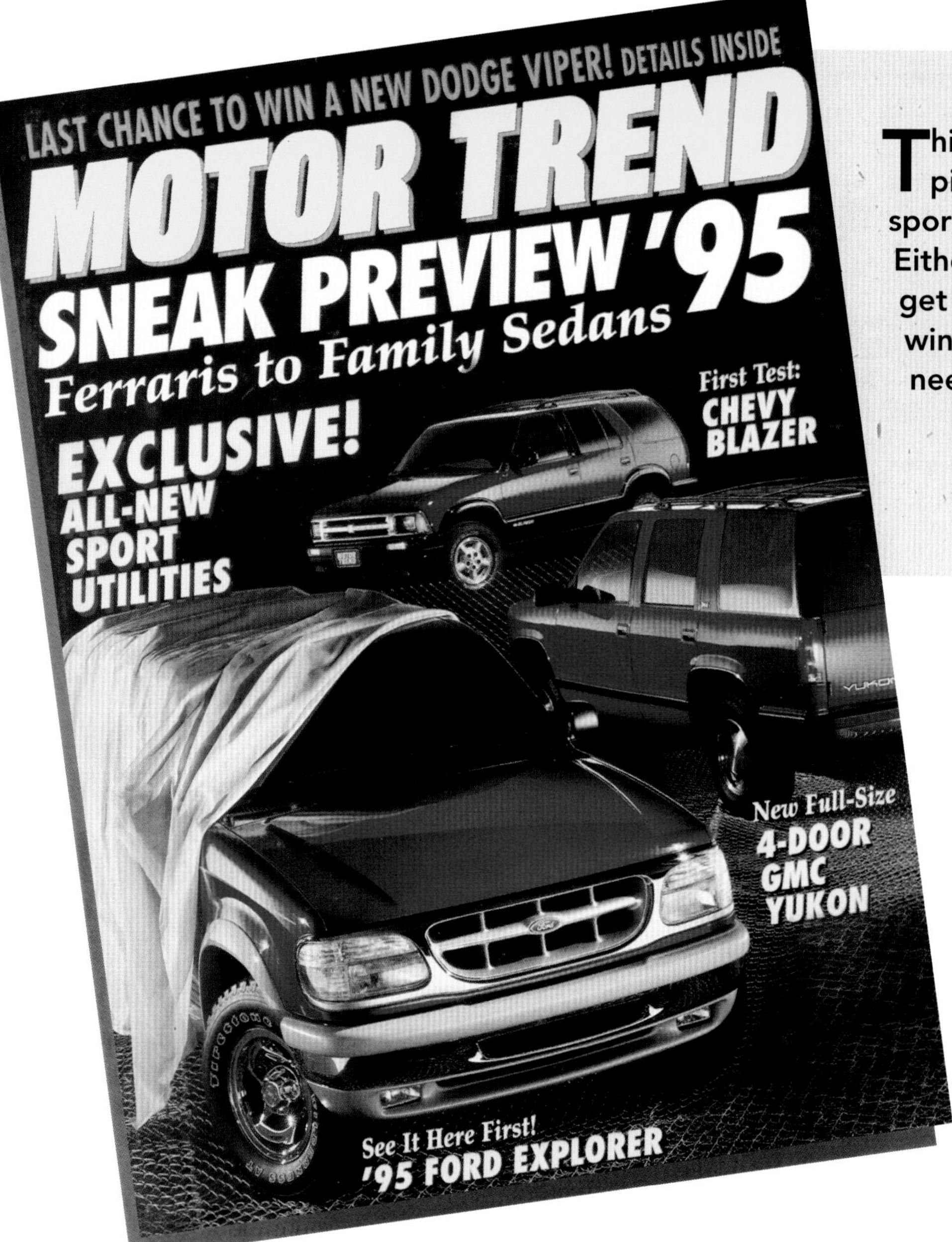

This 1995 Explorer is a grandly impressive piece of work. Most owners buy a sport/utility vehicle for one of two reasons: Either they really need a rugged off roader to get to the cabin or through tough Northern winters—or they just want to look as if they need one for those purposes.

—"1995 Ford Explorer"
September 1994

JANUARY 1994

Motor Trend's 1994 Car of the Year

Ford updated its Mustang for '94 with fresh styling, an updated chassis, and the beloved 5.0-liter/215-horsepower OHV V-8 still under the hood. Known inside Ford by the project code SN95, this basic Mustang would remain in production through '98, and was updated for '99. *"As a stand-alone heir to the Mustang title and throne, the SN95 has pulled the sword from the stone. And in all its iterations, it'll appeal to many more drivers than merely the legion of Mustang buffs who've anxiously awaited its arrival. As an elegant answer to the ponycar equation, the new Mustang earns our highest accolade:* Motor Trend's *'94 Car of the Year."*

1994

APRIL 1994 ▶

The Next Corvette

Motor Trend scooped the world a full three years before the '97 Corvette would appear. Among the things the article got right: the backbone style frame, new V-8, rear-mounted transaxle, and Goodyear run-flat tires. Not all the details were there (including, obviously, the styling), but a follow-up report in 1995 would fill those in.

"The next three years will be filled with wild conjecture about this car, as the hopes and dreams of enthusiasts are projected onto it. Even if only half of the afore-mentioned proves true, the new Corvette will be well worth the wait."

1995

While the next Corvette's envelope is evolutionary in design, the blueprints specify a longer wheelbase, wider track dimensions, and shorter overhangs. Staggered wheel diameters—17-inch in front, 18-inch in back—are planned.

—*"Future Cars, the All New 1998 Corvette"*
April 1995

MAY 1995 ▲

Destination Desolation

Grab three fast European sedans (BMW 540i six-speed, Jaguar XJR, and Mercedes Benz C36), throw in a quick European wagon for kicks (Volvo 850 T-5R), and drive to the most miserable place on earth: California's Death Valley, and the result will be an adventure.

"All too soon, it was time to begin the long trek back to Los Angeles. With careful planning, we devised a route that added hundreds of extra miles to the trip, took us through high-desert cultural centers, such as Nipton (population: seven, including the donkey), and even allowed for a dinner stop back in Baker, under the neon glow of the World's Largest Thermometer (current temperature, 52 degrees Fahrenheit). Over soggy French-dip sandwiches and gut-bombing chocolate shakes, we reached a consensus about our four contenders."

1995

JUNE 1995 ▲

1996 Porsche 911 Turbo

With all-wheel-drive, a twin-turbocharged 3.6-liter SOHC flat-six in its tail sending 400 horsepower out through a six-speed transmission, an unbelievable 3.7-second 0-60 clocking, the latest 911 Turbo was—and may always be—the most astounding air-cooled Porsche ever sold in the United States. It was, for all intents and purposes, a mass-produced 959. And, at about $100,000, a raging bargain.

"The fat tires, all-wheel drive, and suspension upgrades have coalesced in a driving dynamic that is damn near unflappable. The car is unbelievably stable, even in tight downhill, off-camber corners. There's little initial push, and rear breakaway is shockingly gradual. This is the most confident-handling production 911 ever."

JULY 1995 ▲

Ferrari F355 Berlinetta

The Acura NSX put a scare into Ferrari, whose response was the astounding F355. Though sharing basic elements and structure from the disappointing 348, the F355 carried a new 3.5-liter DOHC 40-valve (five per cylinder) V-8 making 375 horsepower at a spine-tingling 8,250 rpm. Thanks to its "flat" crank, it was the best-sounding engine around, as well. The F355 hit 60 in just 4.7 seconds and fileted the quarter-mile in 12.8 seconds at 110.2 mph.

"At $129,500, the F355's rewards for the high-level enthusiast are immense; the sound, feel, ability, and beauty of the car can't be matched at any price. As all great art must, this example reaches deep into the soul of those viewing (or driving) it and elicits passions, memories, and aspirations."

MAY 1995 ▲

American Sport Sedans

With nearly as much power as their musclecar reflections, the 225-horsepower Pontiac Bonneville SE, 220-horsepower Ford Taurus SHO, and 260-horsepower Chevrolet Impala SS were sedan alternatives to performance coupes. But these three cars couldn't have been more distinct; the front-drive Bonneville made its power with a supercharged 3.8-liter OHV V-6; the Taurus SHO drove its front tires with a high-tech, Yamaha-built 3.2-liter DOHC 24-valve V-6; and the big, rear-drive Impala used a Corvette-derived 5.7-liter OHV LT1 V-8. *"The act of choosing a winner among this trio doesn't hinge solely on performance data—each car embodies a decidedly unique, exciting, delicious personality. The Impala SS has character from the bottom of its 17-inch tires to the top of its monochromatic body. Combine that with lowest price and quickest performance of our trio, and the result is a clear victory for Chevrolet. The Bonneville is probably the right choice if you value sophistication over bravado, and fuel economy over tire-melting torque. And though the current Taurus SHO matches the Bonnie on the sophistication scale, fans of the car may be better off waiting for the '96½ iteration to arrive with its promise of V-8 power, roomier interior, improved structure, and superior handling. Any of these cars is more than a match for the American performance sedan of yesteryear—the faster, better handling, and more efficient. In the future, they'll be the standard against which American muscle sedans should be judged."*

1996

One tester began the exercise as a skeptic but came away convinced of nav systems' merits; he summed up his feelings by writing, 'Navigation systems are going to be in the category of How did I live without it, along with cellular phones, home computers, and fax machines.'

—*"Lost or Found?"*
December 1996

1996

AUGUST 1996 ▲

Testing the 467-Horsepower Monte Carlo SS

Chevrolet regularly opens its "Toy Box" to let *Motor Trend* play with marvelous singular concoctions like this rear-drive Monte Carlo overstuffed with a 6.6-liter LT1 V-8 and running a six-speed manual transmission, which ripped to 60 mph in 4.6 seconds and incinerated the quarter-mile in 12.9 seconds at 114.4 mph.

"For a one-off experiment, the fit and finish are excellent, but the structure isn't up to production standards and the brakes need sorting. Relatively speaking, though, if Chevy invested a year of development engineering and installed the upcoming Gen III production V-8, we'd all line up to buy it. Because ultimately, this is a musclecar."

JANUARY 1996 ▲

Driving Ferrari's 333 SP

As wonderful as Ferrari's street vehicles are, it's a company with racing at its very marrow. *MT*'s Michael Brockman got to strap on the 4.0-liter/650-horsepower 60-valve V-12-powered 333 SP used to campaign in and dominate IMSA's World Sports Car series.

"It's the spectacular combination of brilliant cornering, astonishing acceleration, incredible braking, and lack of vibration that makes driving the 333 SP so enthralling. This is probably the best race car I've ever driven."

◄ APRIL 1996

The Family Car Quandary: Sport Utility, Station Wagon, or Minivan?

What type of vehicle is best for a family? Pitting Ford's Explorer XLT V-8 SUV against the Taurus LX wagon and Windstar LX minivan at least gave a clue to befuddled boomers.

"Arguing the merits of these three is much like attempting to determine which is best: running shoes, cowboy boots, or stylish loafers. It's irrelevant that the cowboy boots would doom your chances in the 100-meter dash, or that the loafers would spoil your prospects in a line-dancing competition. Just as with footwear, each of these has distinct benefits and drawbacks. In the final analysis, considering the Windstar's huge edge in functionality, the minivan seems a runaway winner in family values."

1997

Perhaps more surprising than its tectonic-plate-shifting power is the refined character of the Venom 600 GTS. Around town the 514-cubic-inch engine idles smoothly, refusing to overheat or otherwise misbehave. Under mild acceleration, the car behaves almost benignly, at least within the realm of Vipers. However, a romp on the loud pedal awakens the sleeping beast like a red-hot poker.

—"Hennessey Venom 600 GTS"
December 1997

JANUARY 1997

Speed Blind

The new BMW 5 Series was *Motor Trend's* 1997 Import Car of the Year, and Editor C. Van Tune traveled to Germany to pick up the magazine's long-term 540i six-speed.

"Throttle to the floor and four-cam V-8 at full song, the nasty black BMW's speedometer needle swept past 155 mph as the tach became buried in the red zone. That's fifth gear, with one more to go, boys. Ahead, the vast German autobahn stretched out in front of me like an unfurling ribbon to dementia. Speed is as addictive as any drug, and the craving for more, stronger doses soon becomes impossible to resist. I'm as busy as hell right about now, however, with one hand on the wheel and the other balancing a camera. Click . . . flash . . . and there's our lead photo."

1997

JANUARY 1997 ▲

Road Test: General Motors EV1

There's never been a more advanced electric vehicle than GM's EV1. To explore its ability, *MT* sent Jeff Bartlett out to drive it as GM recommends and John Pearley Huffman to drive it like a regular car. The car's limitations have kept it from being adopted in great numbers. *"Today, driving is rarely an adventure. Short of crashing, not much bad can happen. Run out of gas? Walk a block to the Shell station. Flat tire? Call AAA. Blow a head gasket? Use the 50,000-mile warranty. All that is thrown out the window, however, with GM's brilliant EV1 electric car now available for purchase (well, for lease) by Mr. and Mrs. America."*

1997

1997

◂ FEBRUARY 1997

First Photos—First Test: 1997 Corvette!

Three years after *MT's* first report on its engineering and development, it was finally time to drive the C5 Corvette with its new 5.7-liter/345-horsepower all-aluminum OHV LS1 V-8, rear-mounted six-speed transaxle, and vastly improved structure and practicality. So good would the C5 prove to be that it would be named *MT's* '98 Car of the Year one year after this first test.

"Acceleration testing showed 0-60 mph in 4.7 seconds and the quarter mile in 13.3 seconds at 106.8 mph. On the track, the Corvette proved to be a fire-breathing demon with good common sense—a superfast playtoy insured by Mutual of Heaven."

JULY 1997 ▴

Mercedes-Benz SLK230 and 1971 280SL

Mercedes' new SLK230 used a supercharged 2.3-liter DOHC 16-valve four making 191 horsepower to fling itself to 60 mph in just 6.9 seconds. But the real thrill of the car lay in its handsome styling, delicately detailed interior, and a power hardtop that retracts amusingly with one button. And next to the classic 280SL, its heritage was obvious.

"Like its latter-day SL kin, the SLK forgoes the kind of adrenaline-pumping, bang-through-the-gears excitement of, for instance, the Porsche Boxster—or 300SL—for a more civilized and refined character (like that of the 280SL). That said, drive one down the boulevard, and the turning heads will have you wondering if there are any other sports cars on the street."

1998

The result of many months of clandestine research and contacting just the right people reveals what the automakers don't dare disclose to each other. The following pages unveil the secret vehicles they have been working on—uncovered now for your eyes only.

—*"Future Cars, Look Into the Crystal Ball of Automotive Design"*
April 1998

FEBRUARY 1998 ▲

1999 Lexus RX 300

The commingling of truck and car design reached its apex with the Lexus RX 300—a full-fledged all-wheel-drive SUV based on a car component set. So ground-breaking is the RX 300 that when it became eligible for MT's "of the Year" consideration, a new award was cast for it. The RX 300 became *Motor Trend's* first "Sport/Utility of the Year" in '99. *"There's considerable band width in the SUV spectrum between 'truckish' and 'carlike.' Mercedes splices the M-Class with an excellent balance of truck and luxury car DNA, but the Lexus moves even further toward the luxury car side of the formula."*

1998

◄ JANUARY 1998

First Look: Volkswagen's New Beetle

It undeniably looks like a Beetle, but underneath, the skin is pure VW Golf IV. The revolutionary aspect of the Beetle isn't in the way it works (it's a front-driver powered by a 2.0-liter four—what could be more common?), but in how it's built. The ultimate stretch of production flexibility allows Volkswagen to build a niche, almost whimsical, vehicle off a basic platform. For the daring and bravado of its design, the Beetle earned *MT's* '99 Import Car of the Year honor.

"Time will be the ultimate arbiter as to whether America embraces this automotive second coming as enthusiastically as it did the first time around. But our initial encounter with the intriguing New Beetle leads us to believe it will have more than a fighting chance for a long and successful run."

NOVEMBER 1998 ►

Shelby Series 1

Carroll Shelby knows how to push *Motor Trend's* editorial hot button. The appearance of the new Shelby Series 1 roadster, with power from a 320-horsepower version of Oldsmobile's 4.0-liter DOHC 32-valve Aurora V-8.

"Don't think this is a car designed by some new-age GM marketing committee. This is Carroll's baby through and through. The frame: designed and built by Shelby American and its engineering partners. The body: the same. The suspension: ditto. The interior: yeah, you got it. The overall size, shape, look, and purpose: all Shelby, all the time."

1999

Go ahead, drag race an IRL car 0-60 mph. You'll win. Challenge a Winston Cup car in the quarter mile, you'll beat it. Go up against the world's best-handling production vehicles on a slalom course. You'll spank 'em. Then head to the skid-pad and you'll again embarrass them red. This is one bad-ass, walk-the-walk, talk-the-talk street-fighter. A 650-horse street-legal Viper that looks every other car straight in the headlights and dares, 'C'mon, try me!'

—"The Fastest Street Car We've Ever Tested"
June 1999

JUNE 1999

Wide Bloody Open

Motor Trend's sponsorship of the Price Cobb Racing's Infiniti-powered IRL Indy Car made a test of the 730-horsepower 1,833-pound racer inevitable. Zero to 60? 3.8 seconds. Quarter-mile? 10.6 seconds at 153.7 mph. On the high banks of Texas Motor Speedway? It laps the oval at an average of nearly 220 mph.

"Going through the Texas banking at 200 mph is like being miniaturized and going for a ride in a tethered gas-powered model airplane, while inside a gymnasium: If the wire breaks, the resulting crash wouldn't be pretty."

1999

MARCH 1999 ▲

Yesterday and Today: Ford Mustangs

Ford's Mustang went through yet another updating for '99, with the GT model's 4.6-liter SOHC V-8 now pumping out 260 horsepower. Why not pit it against the legendary 335-horsepower '69 Mach 1 428 Cobra Jet and George Follmer's 470-horsepower '69 Boss 302 Trans Am racer? And why not have George Follmer himself there to lend perspective? *"Packing up his driving suit, Follmer pauses to summarize: 'Cobra Jets, 302s, all the variety of engine and horsepower combinations that Ford has installed in the Mustang over the years are just phenomenal. Even though it's a smaller engine now, and in spite of all the government bureaucracy that has come down over time, Ford has produced a fun car that has some kick-in-the-butt."*

Index